EXTRA! EXTRA!
Read All About It!

Using the Daily News for Reading Practice

by Walter A. Hazen

Rigby Best Teachers Press

An imprint of Rigby • A division of Reed Elsevier, Inc.

Dedication

To Martha, Jordan, and Allison

Acknowledgements

I would like to thank Laura Strom for giving me the opportunity to work on this book, as well as Georgine Cooper, who very ably guided me through it.

The following are reprinted by permission:

© Culver Pictures, p. 12; © The Granger Collection, New York, p. 13; © 1912 by the New York Times Company. Reprinted with permission, p. 20; © 1994 by the New York Times Company. Reprinted with permission, p. 26; © Corbis, p. 50; Approved by Mark Silverman, Publisher and Editor, for Detroit News reprints only. "Reprinted with permission from The Detroit News," pp. 58, 67; © AP/Wide World, pp. 72; © The Granger Collection, New York, p. 116; © Detroit Free Press, p. 124.

For more information about other books from Rigby Best Teachers Press, please contact Rigby at 800 822-8661 or **www.rigby.com**

Editor: Georgine Cooper
Designer: Sean O'Neill, Ronan Design
Cover Illustrator: Johnna Bandle
Executive Editor: Laura Strom
Design Project Manager: Tom Sjoerdsma

Table of Contents

 =
Reproducible Page

© 2001 Rigby

Table of Contents

Table of Contents

INTRODUCTION

To many readers, the daily newspaper is simply a disposable record of recent news and events. They peruse the front page, skim the sections on national and local news, glance at the comics and sports pages, and may even have a go at the puzzle. Then, without a second thought, they consign the paper to the recycling bin.

Many teachers see newspapers in a different light. They recognize that the newspaper is a valuable resource that can be used as an instructional resource for a variety of subjects—reading, social studies, math, or science, for example. They know that each section of the newspaper offers ways to reinforce or enhance skills that will serve students throughout their formal education and their lives. And they realize that the newspaper, at a cost of a few cents a day, is one of the most inexpensive and readily available resources at their fingertips.

In *Extra! Extra! Read All About It!*, teachers will find many suggestions for using the newspaper in the classroom. The activities in this book can be used sequentially or independently, depending on the available time and your needs. Chapters on the various newspaper sections include reproducible activities to motivate even reluctant readers. The front page, the editorial page, classified ads, local and national news, and even the sports and comics pages, are among the sections featured.

Each chapter contains several activities focusing on such skills as fact and opinion, synonyms and antonyms, writing, spelling, and identifying the 5 Ws—*who*, *what*, *where*, *when*, and *why*—of lead paragraphs. Some of the activities are used within the framework of guided reading.

It is important to have an ample supply of newspapers readily available to students. If your school has a subscription to one or more newspapers, you will have a convenient supply. You may also ask students to bring papers from home—after the family has read them, of course. Many newspapers have online editions; you can access papers from all over the world through the Internet. (See page 133 for some major newspaper websites.)

Don't forget to preview materials for age and content appropriateness before your students have access. If students bring newspapers or articles from home, preview these before students share them with the class.

I hope that the suggestions and activities presented in *Extra! Extra! Read All About It!* will help teachers transform students into avid readers who have added another rich resource to their reading repertoire.

Walter A. Hazen

CHAPTER ONE

The Newspaper Adventure

TEACHER USES NEWSPAPER TO TEACH READING AND WRITING

So you've decided to use the newspaper as an aid in improving the reading and writing skills of your students. Smart decision! The information contained in the newspaper can enhance the ability of avid readers and go far to motivate those for whom reading is not a preferred activity. Where else in but a few pages can students read about everything from presidents to bungee jumpers or catch up on recent world events, be they happening in the Persian Gulf or in Sherman's Lagoon? And while they are improving their reading skills, students are broadening their knowledge of the world in which they live.

It should be relatively easy to acquire a ready supply of current newspapers for students to use. Many families subscribe to a daily newspaper and would gladly share their copies with the school. Many newspapers have special programs that enable schools to have subscriptions at an affordable cost. Most major newspapers also make editions available online.

Reproductions of classic advertisements that appear throughout the book provide an interesting visual history of the newspapers and the times.

For your convenience, reproducible pages are noted with the ℞℞℞ symbol.

To begin your newspaper adventure, this chapter contains a brief, reproducible history and some warm-up activities.

A Brief History of the Newspaper

FIRST NEWSPAPERS PUBLISHED ANYWHERE

Many people are surprised to learn that the modern newspaper, in broad historical terms, is a relatively recent innovation. Although the ancient Romans posted government news in public announcements called the *Acta Diurna*, or *Acts of the Day*, the newspaper as it eventually evolved did not appear until around 1440 when Johannes Gutenberg invented the printing press with movable type.

Sources differ as to what constituted the first real newspaper. Some grant that distinction to a German publication called *Avista Relation oder Zeitung*, which appeared in 1609. Others maintain that the *Weekly Newes*, an English newspaper founded in 1622, was the first. Still others argue that the *Oxford Gazette*, another English publication introduced in 1665, rightly deserves that recognition. Actually, the editor of the *Oxford Gazette* was the first to use the word *newspaper* in describing his weekly publication.

A reproduction of the front page of the October 31, 1765, *The Pennsylvania Journal and Weekly Advertiser*.

NEWSPAPERS COME TO UNITED STATES

Newspapers in America got off to a rough start. The first one, in fact, was suppressed after its first issue on September 25, 1690. It was called *Publick Occurrences Both Foreign and Domestick*. Its founder, Benjamin Harris of Boston, had earlier gotten into trouble in England for criticizing the king and had to flee the country. In America he angered Simon Bradstreet, the Royal Governor of Massachusetts, by making disparaging remarks about him. As a result, Bradstreet shut down the newspaper after the first issue. No other newspapers appeared for the rest of the century.

The next American newspaper to appear was the *Boston News-Letter*. It was published on a regular basis from 1704 until the Revolutionary War. Begun by John Campbell, it received the blessing of the authorities on the condition that it did not print anything objectionable to the King of England or the Colonial government.

Other newspapers followed. One of particular interest was the *New England Courant*, another Boston publication, founded by James Franklin in 1721. When James was imprisoned for boldly hinting that members of the Massachusetts legislature had accepted bribes from coastal pirates, his sixteen-year-old brother Benjamin took over the operation of the newspaper. This is the same Benjamin Franklin who later achieved fame as a printer, historian, diplomat, and scientist.

Were Colonial newspapers published only in Boston? Did the rest of Colonial America go about in the dark? That was certainly not the case. In 1719, Andrew Bradford founded the *American Weekly Mercury* in Philadelphia. Other weekly newspapers —later known as weeklies—followed. By the time of the American Revolution, approximately thirty-five newspapers were being published on a regular basis. By 1760, all the colonies except Delaware and New Jersey had at least one.

Unlike our modern editions, early newspapers actually contained very little of what we now consider news. They focused mostly on business and politics. Also unlike our modern editions, they generally ignored other news that might have interested the local people.

Newspapers were also expensive for the time. The average newspaper cost about six cents—a lot of money for a family who struggled to put food on the table. And anyone who could afford the price got very little for the money. Some early newspapers consisted of only one page, although the average length for a weekly was four pages.

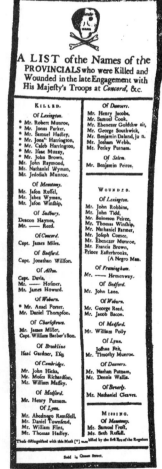

A list of colonists killed in the battle of Concord in the American Revolution from the archives of the Library of Congress.

"Join, or Die," America's first political cartoon, was created in 1754 by Benjamin Franklin for his *Pennsylvania Gazette*.

STUDENT CHALLENGE

Before proceeding with Part Two of the brief history, challenge your students with an activity that involves critical thinking and writing. The activity on page 11 involves support of a position against a government order—an opinion that we have the right to express now, but would have been dangerous to express then. **Write a Letter to the Royal Governor** gives students an opportunity to petition the Royal Governor of Massachusetts in support of Benjamin Harris's newspaper and to give reasons why they do. Such an activity provides an opportunity for students to examine an issue.

Once you have finished Part Two of the history, use the **Fill in a Venn Diagram** activity on page 19 to compare early newspapers with today's editions and the **Complete a Newspaper Timeline** on page 18. They can be used as an individual, partner, or group activity.

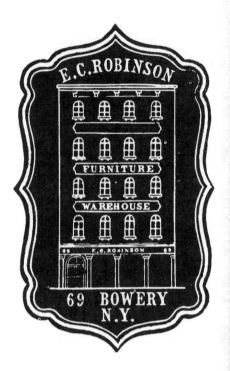

Name _____

Write a Letter to the Royal Governor

Pretend you are living in the year 1690.

Write a letter to Simon Bradstreet, the Royal Governor of Massachusetts, in support of Benjamin Harris and his newspaper, *Publick Occurrences Both Foreign and Domestick.*

Give three reasons why you feel that the British Crown should not dictate what is printed in colonial newspapers.

Use the back of this page or an extra sheet of paper if necessary.

October 1, 1690

Governor Simon Bradstreet

Boston, Massachusetts

Your Excellency:

I strongly disagree with your decision to shut down Benjamin Harris's newspaper.

First,

Next,

Finally,

Sincerely,

(sign your name)

A Brief History of the Newspaper

POPULAR PENNY PAPERS PROPAGATED

Newspapers remained inaccessible to most people until 1833, when Benjamin H. Day founded the *New York Sun*. The *Sun* was the first penny newspaper to appear in the United States. Others soon followed, giving the reading public not only an affordable publication, but one that was lively and entertaining. Penny newspapers were the first to provide readers with news and events of local interest. Buyers could hardly wait to search the pages and learn about the latest gossip and happenings in their town or neighborhood.

Many newspapers that later became American traditions had their beginnings as penny papers. The *New York Tribune*, founded in 1841 by Horace Greeley, and the *New York Times*, founded ten years later by Henry J. Raymond, began this way. So did Joseph Pulitzer's *St. Louis Dispatch* and a host of others. Penny newspapers were in their heyday in the decades between the 1830s and 1880s.

In the period between 1880 and 1890, the bigger and faster presses of the late 1800s enabled publishers to increase circulation. Also at this time, photographs began to appear in newspapers.

The front page of the first issue of the *New York Sun*, September 3, 1833, the first successful penny daily, founded by Benjamin H. Day.

"YELLOW JOURNALISM" SPREADS ACROSS NATION

As more newspapers appeared and competition became keen, publishers found that local news and gossip were not enough to ensure a high volume of sales. They started turning to what became known as "yellow journalism," the reporting of sensational news stories that stretched the truth to the limit. Many times there was little or no truth at all in them.

Yellow journalism is a term derived from a comic strip character named "The Yellow Kid." The Kid was a street urchin in a yellow nightshirt created by artist Richard Outcast. He first appeared in a newspaper in 1896 in Joseph Pulitzer's *New York World* in a cartoon known as "Hogan's Alley." The cartoon became such a success that William Randolph Hearst, publisher of the rival *New York Journal*, lured Outcast away from the *World* to draw the funny-looking kid for his own paper. When this happened, the *World* hired another artist to draw a competing Yellow Kid. What began simply as two newspapers using a cartoon character to increase sales soon mushroomed into a heated rivalry to publish the most sordid and sensational news stories. Because of the Yellow Kid, the printing of such stories came to be called "yellow journalism."

At no period in our history was yellow journalism more popular than during the Spanish-American War. Both the *New York World* and the *New York Journal* featured headlines and stories about supposed Spanish atrocities in Cuba. According to reporters, blood was everywhere: on the roadsides, in the fields, and on the doorsteps. When artist Frederic Remington, working for Hearst's *Journal*, telegraphed his publisher that he found little going on in Cuba, Hearst shot back: "You furnish the pictures; I'll furnish the war!" And so it went; much of the material printed in the newspapers was written by reporters who never left their Havana hotels.

Comic strip by R. F. Outcault for the *New York World*, 1896, featuring one of his most famous characters, The Yellow Kid.

NUMBER OF NEWS DAILIES GROWS

The number of daily newspapers increased steadily until about 1920, when there were more than 2,000 in circulation in America. Then a gradual decline occurred over the next half century. New techniques and machines that made printing more efficient also made it more expensive, resulting in mergers, consolidations, and chains. The six largest newspaper companies today are Gannett, Knight-Ridder, Newhouse, Dow Jones and Company, Times Mirror, and the New York Times Company. The advent of television in the 1950s also contributed to the decrease in the number of papers.

In the 1970s and 1980s, computer technology had a great impact on the ways newspapers were produced. In the 1990s reporters could send stories from around the world almost instantly using laptop computers and modems and many newspapers made online editions available on the Internet.

As of 1997, there were about 1500 daily newspapers being published in the United States. Of this number, roughly 800 are afternoon publications, while 700 are morning papers. Only 12 newspapers put out both a morning and afternoon edition. In contrast, the number of weekly newspapers has remained constant at between 7,000 and 8,000.

Recent years have also seen a tremendous decline in the number of rival newspapers. At the turn of the century, most major cities had competing publications. Today, competing newspapers are found in less than 50 cities. There has also been a decline in the number of people who read a daily newspaper. Today, about 59% of Americans say they read the newspaper everyday. The number of readers is a little higher for Sunday editions.

"Chequing" the American Traveler

A million miles of *sunshine* in TUCSON ("Too-sŏhn")

Manicuring

WHO READS NEWSPAPERS TODAY?

So who in the general population reads newspapers? As a rule, readership is highest among older Americans and those with higher incomes. Almost 70% of people over the age of 69 reads a newspaper every day. This percentage drops to less than 50% in the 18–24 range. These statistics suggest that people below the age of 24 get their news from another source—such as television, radio, or the Internet—or pay less attention to the news.

Regardless of age, few people sit down and read an entire newspaper. Some only glance at the headlines, then hurry to the sports or comics sections. Others may be interested only in local events or entertainment news. With this in mind, ask your students to do the **Conduct a Survey about Newspaper Readership** activity on pages 16 and 17.

The **Complete a Newspaper Timeline** activity on page 18 provides an opportunity to revisit the "Brief History" and check comprehension.

The **Fill in a Venn Diagram** activity provides an opportunity to compare and contrast early American newspapers with those of today.

Name _____

Conduct a Survey About Newspaper Readership

Choose three people in your school or neighborhood to interview about their newspaper reading habits.

Ask them the questions listed on these pages.

If possible, select people of varying ages and backgrounds, as these factors sometimes determine what they read.

Use the back of this sheet or an extra sheet of paper if you need more writing room.

BAKER.

Person #1: Name .... Age (optional) ....

Person #2: Name .... Age (optional) ....

Person #3: Name .... Age (optional) ....

1. Which newspaper(s) do you read or subscribe to?

Person #1: ....

Person #2: ....

Person #3: ....

2. Which part(s) of the newspaper do you enjoy the most?

Person #1: ....

....

Person #2: ....

....

Person #3: ....

....

3. Which part(s) of the newspaper do you seldom or never read? Why?

Person #1: ....

....

Person #2: ....

....

Person #3: ....

....

 Rigby Best Teachers Press

4. Approximately how many minutes a day do you devote to reading the newspaper?

Person #1:

Person #2:

Person #3:

5. What improvements, if any, should the publisher make to your newspaper?

Person #1:

Person #2:

Person #3:

6. Would you rate your newspaper "Good," "Fair," or "Poor?" Why?

Person #1:

Person #2:

Person #3:

Name _____

Complete a Newspaper Timeline

Using "A Brief History of the Newspaper," fill in the timeline below.

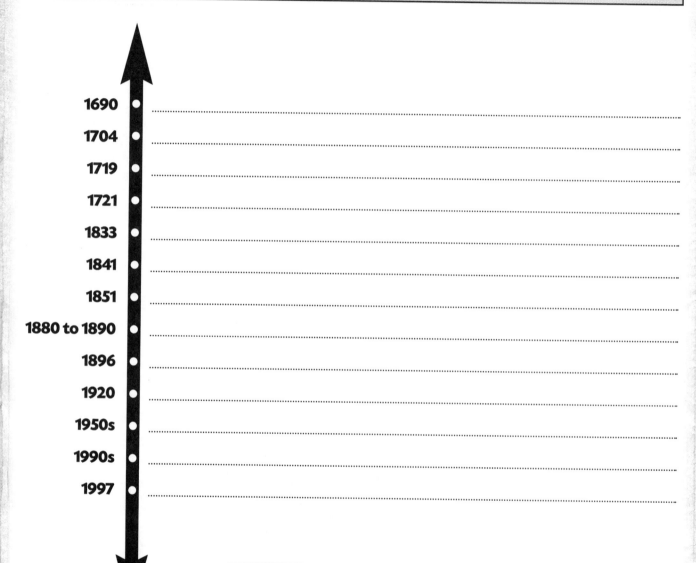

1690 ....

1704 ....

1719 ....

1721 ....

1833 ....

1841 ....

1851 ....

1880 to 1890 ....

1896 ....

1920 ....

1950s ....

1990s ....

1997 ....

Name _____

Fill in a Venn Diagram

Fill in the Venn diagram below to compare early newspapers with those of today. Write facts about each in the appropriate place. List features common to both where the circles overlap.

    Use "A Brief History of the Newspaper," encyclopedias, library books, or Internet resources for reference.

Early Newspapers   **Modern Newspapers**

Both

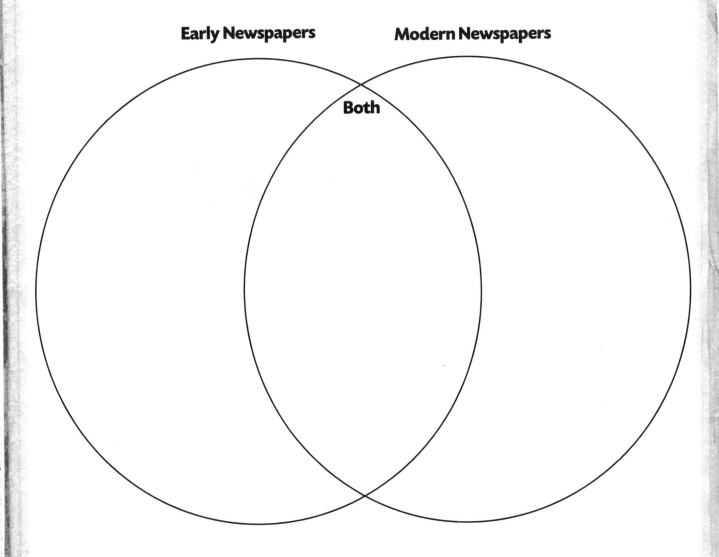

CHAPTER TWO

The Front Page and the News

FRONT PAGE MOST IMPORTANT PART OF PAPER, EXPERTS SAY

When people who are either very busy or not very interested pick up a newspaper, the part most likely to capture their attention is the front page. A quick perusal of it will tell them whether the Martians have landed or if Bigfoot was indeed seen trying on sneakers at a Sacramento shoe store.

Because many readers buy newspapers from either vending machines or across store counters, the front page must be attractive and capable of catching the prospective buyer's eye. The front page is the most important part of a newspaper. In effect, it serves as a daily window to the world, giving readers a concise rundown of significant world, national, and regional events that might impact their lives. With this in mind, editors carefully

The front page of *The New York Times*, April 16, 1912.

©2001 Rigby

choose the stories and materials that they print on page one.

The first activity in this chapter, **Explore Your News Knowledge**, is designed to explore with your students what they know about a newspaper's front page. **Fill in a Venn Diagram** asks students to compare the components of the front pages of two newspapers. **Practicing with Headlines** gives practice in making complete sentences, restating, and identifying parts of speech in headlines. **Dissecting Front Page News** allows students to demonstrate comprehension of a major news story.

STUDENT CHALLENGE

Ask the questions below as a launching point for **Explore Your News Knowledge**

• Make an overhead of the **Explore Your News Knowledge** reproducible or distribute copies to students.

• Add other questions that arise during your exploration.

• Have samples of the front page from a variety of daily newspapers available for reference.

• Ask one or more students to record responses on the board.

1. What items can be found on the front page of a newspaper? Answers will vary. Some students are sure to point out that the front page highlights the most important news stories of the day. Others might add that a brief synopsis of the weather is also likely to appear on page one. Those more familiar with the newspaper might volunteer that the front page further serves as a guide to what is inside the paper. If not, point out that the front page often contains a small heading entitled "Inside" or "Index" that is similar to a table of contents. Distribute copies of front pages to pairs or small groups of students. After they have had a few minutes to examine them, see if they would like to add items to their list.

2. *What is meant by "news?"* Ask students to define "news" in their own words; then reference a dictionary. "A report of recent events" and "previously unknown information" (*Merriam-Webster's Collegiate Dictionary*, Tenth Edition, 1999) are common definitions. News is also defined as something reported in the newspaper or other news source. Explain that what is news to one person may not be news to another. Ask your students whether they agree or disagree with this definition.

3. *Is the following incident "news?" Why or why not?*

On the way to his wedding, the groom's car stalled on a flooded street. As a result, he missed the wedding entirely and left his bride sobbing at the altar and relatives on both sides fighting.

Is news anything that is of interest to people? If this is not news, what would make it news? Answers will vary and might include for example, if "it involves well-known people," "things got violent," or "anyone was arrested."

Once you have agreed on a workable definition of "news," review the headlines that appear on the front page of today's or a recent newspaper and evaluate the newsworthiness of the stories.

4. *Are the headlines in complete sentences? Why are they written this way?*

Answers will vary. Most students will recognize that headlines are fragments and that they are short to grab attention.

> *OPTIONAL ACTIVITY:*
> Have students point out errors in spelling and grammar in the stories they read.

Name _____

Explore Your News Knowledge

What items can be found on the front page of a newspaper?

....

....

....

....

What is meant by the word *news*?

....

....

....

....

Is the following incident news? Why or why not?

On the way to his wedding, the groom's car stalled on a flooded street. As a result, he missed the wedding entirely and left his bride sobbing at the altar and relatives on both sides fighting.

....

....

....

....

Are the headlines in complete sentences? Why are they written this way?

....

....

....

Name _____

Fill in a Venn Diagram

Look at the front page of two different newspapers. Somewhere at either the top or the bottom is a list or table of contents with page numbers that tells the reader what features are included within. Compare the contents of the papers and fill in the Venn diagram below. Write facts about each in the appropriate place. List features common to both where the circles overlap.

First Newspaper   **Second Newspaper**

Both

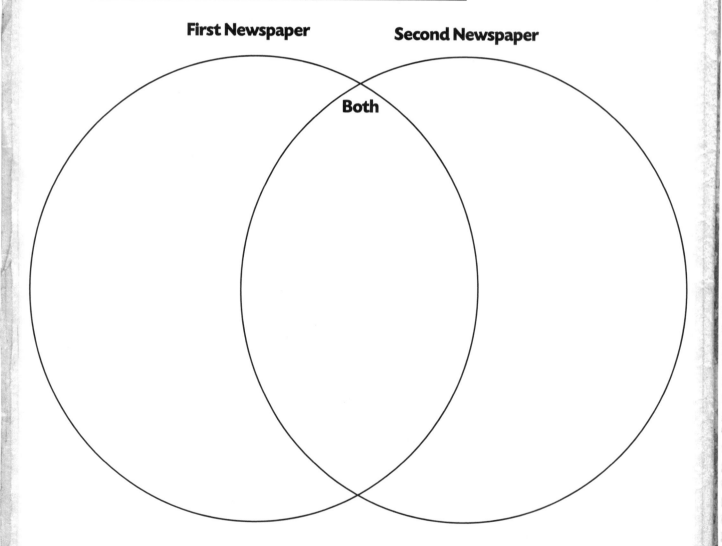

Name _____

Practicing with Headlines

Use the front page of a newspaper to do the following:

1. Choose three headlines and write them on the lines below.

....

....

....

....

....

2. Rewrite the headlines to make them complete sentences.

....

....

....

....

....

3. Label the nouns, verbs, adjectives, and adverbs in the sentences you have written for number 2. Use N for noun, V for verb, Adj for adjective, and Adv for adverb.

4. Create a new headline for each of the three you chose in number 1.

....

....

....

....

....

ELEMENTS OF A NEWS STORY DISCOVERED

After exploring the concept of news and analyzing headlines with students, it's time to delve into the stories or articles. Discuss with students the "5 Ws"—*who, what, where, when, why*—as well as the *how* of news stories. Review your exploration of what makes a story front page news. Before having students complete **Dissecting Front Page News** independently, practice doing this together.

• Select a short, front page article to model.

• Make an overhead of the **Dissecting Front Page News** reproducible or distribute copies to the students.

• Read or ask a student to read the article aloud.

• Have students respond orally, or ask one or more students to record responses.

• Have available appropriate, pre-selected front page articles clipped from a newspaper or printed out from an online newspaper.

You may assign specific articles or allow students to choose.

• Have students complete the activity individually, in pairs, or in groups.

OPTIONAL ACTIVITY: Have students present their "dissections" to the class.

The front page of *The New York Times*, May 11, 1994.

Name _____

Dissecting Front Page News

Read a news article; then answer the questions and do the items below.

1. Write the headline from the article. Was it a fragment or a complete sentence?

....

2. Who are the important people in the story?

....

....

3. When did the story take place?

....

....

4. Where did the story take place? Was the story local, national, or international in nature?

....

....

....

5. What happened in the story? Write a brief summary.

....

....

6. Why do you think this article appeared on the front page?

....

....

7. Did you find any unfamiliar vocabulary words in the article? Write them on the
   lines below. Use the back of this sheet if you need more room. Can you guess the meaning from
   the context? Write the definition of each word. Use a dictionary if you need help.

....

....

....

LOST DOG FOUND SLEEPING IN NEIGHBOR'S GARAGE

There are often interesting articles that readers overlook because they are confined to the inner depths of a newspaper. Write the following headline for a news brief on the chalkboard and ask your students to determine why it never made it to the front page.

Lost Dog Found Sleeping in Neighbor's Garage.

• Ask, *"Why wouldn't this be front page news?"*

Answers will vary, but most students respond that there is nothing unusual about a lost dog turning up at a neighbor's house.

• Ask, *"What would make this front page news?"*

Again, answers will vary but may include things like "if the garage was locked and the neighbor wasn't home" or if it was a former neighbor who lived in another state."

• Select other brief news items from the inside of a current newspaper and ask your students to determine why such stories appeared on the inside pages, rather than the front page. Also ask if any of the stories might have appeared on the front page of a newspaper in another city.

• Distribute **The Anywhere Tribune** report.

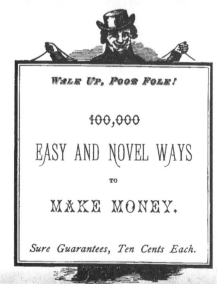

Name _____

The Anywhere Tribune

SCIENTISTS GROW HAIR ON BOWLING BALL

You are a star reporter for *The Anywhere Tribune*.

Write a front page article for the headline "Scientists grow hair on a bowling ball." (Hint: Does this mean hope is just around the corner for the hairless?)

Be sure to include answers to the 5 Ws—*Who? What? When? Where?* and *Why?*

GROUP EXPLORATION OF TOPIC SENTENCE LAUNCHED

How well do your students understand the stories they read? Can they identify the topic sentences and main ideas? These are two indicators of comprehension.

The topic sentence is often the first sentence in a news story. However, this is not always the case. For example, in a feature story the topic sentence might just as easily be at the end of a paragraph or even in the middle.

At right are two versions of the same paragraph with the topic sentence (in italics) in different places. Reproduce copies for each student or copy onto an overhead. Reference the paragraphs in a discussion about topic sentence, main idea, and supporting sentences. Students can easily see that all sentences in the above paragraphs relate to the one sentence stating that the residents of the 800 block of Elm street are sprucing up their neighborhood. Although the topic sentences of some paragraphs are more difficult to pinpoint and are sometimes only implied, the sooner the reader identifies these the easier it will be to understand the article.

After the group exploration of topic sentences, distribute the **Identify Topic Sentences** reproducible on pages 31 and 32. Have students work individually, in groups, or in pairs, then share their responses with the class.

LOCAL NEIGHBORHOOD GETS FACE-LIFT FROM RESIDENTS

Residents of the 800 block of Elm Street are sprucing up their neighborhood. Houses that have not seen a coat of paint in decades are being transformed into topics of conversation for passersby. Roofs that have surely leaked for years are suddenly sporting new shingles, and cracked and broken windowpanes are gradually being replaced. Even lawns are undergoing face-lifts; weeds are disappearing and plugs and sprigs of grass are slowly taking their place.

Houses that have not seen a coat of paint in decades are being transformed into topics of conversation for passersby. Roofs that have surely leaked for years are suddenly sporting new shingles, and cracked and broken windowpanes are gradually being replaced. Even lawns are undergoing face-lifts; weeds are disappearing and plugs and sprigs of grass are slowly taking their place. *Residents of the 800 block of Elm Street are sprucing up their neighborhood.*

Name _____

Identify Topic Sentences

On these two pages are several paragraphs that might have been part of stories on the main page of any local newspaper. Read each carefully, and, on the lines provided, write its topic sentence. Remember that the topic sentence may appear anywhere in a feature story.

Traffic in both directions came to a complete stop. People leaned from car windows to get a better look, adults smiling and children shrieking with delight. Even though the traffic light turned green, no one moved or honked a horn. Everyone seemed enthralled at the sight of the mother duck and her four fluffy ducklings waddling across the intersection.

Topic Sentence:

....

....

....

....

BEAUTY

OUTLOOKING

TOWARD

HOPE'S LAND

OF

PROMISE.

Democratic candidate Yancy Yakker isn't difficult to spot. At 6'8", he hovers above the crowd, causing children and others who are shorter to develop neck pains just looking up at him. Not to be overlooked is his booming voice, which jars sleepers to attention and sends babies into fits of crying. And then there is that fire–truck–red blazer he usually wears. "Once a Georgia Bulldog, always a Georgia Bulldog," he likes to say.

Topic Sentence:

....

....

....

....

Name _____

Identify Topic Sentences

At right are two paragraphs that might have been part of stories on the main page of any local newspaper. Read each carefully, and, on the lines provided, write its topic sentence. Remember that the topic sentence may appear anywhere in a feature story.

VACATIONS FOR SALE CHEAP! *in the* **WEST**

One wing of the small plane rested against Farmer Brown's barn. The other lay in an adjacent field. Daredevil Dan, the plane's pilot, was lucky to be alive. This was especially true considering he was thrown 10 feet from the crash sight and landed dangerously close to Farmer Brown's prize bull, which was grazing nearby.

Topic Sentence:

_____

_____

_____

_____

The storm wreaked havoc on the downtown area. Power lines were down in many places and tree limbs littered the streets. A number of store windows were blown out and several cars sustained damage from the golf ball-size hail that accompanied the heavy rain.

Topic Sentence:

_____

_____

_____

_____

IMPLIED MAIN IDEA DOUBLES AS TOPIC SENTENCE

In the **Identify Topic Sentences** activity, the topic sentences are fairly easy to find. Sometimes, however, the main idea is not stated; it is implied. The **Adding a Topic Sentence** reproducible contains samples of two paragraphs in which the latter is the case. Use this activity to practice making inferences.

• Make an overhead of the **Adding a Topic Sentence** reproducible or distribute copies to the students.
• Read and discuss them one at a time with the class.
• Tell students they will write a topic sentence for each paragraph on the line below it.

• Tell them to draw an arrow from the topic sentence to the place it belongs in the paragraph.

For the first paragraph, ask, "Is there a topic sentence in the first paragraph?" Ask, "What is the main idea?" "People support Senator Yakker for a variety of reasons," is the main idea. If it were stated in the paragraph, it would be the topic sentence. Discuss that all the sentences support this main idea—even though it isn't stated.

Tell students that the second paragraph is the one about the ducks crossing the road. This time, however, the last—the topic— sentence has been left out. Ask them to create a new topic sentence that would explain why the traffic stopped and to write it on the line below the paragraph.

WINDOW CLEANING

Name _____

Adding a Topic Sentence

Write a topic sentence for each article below.

THOMPSON'S
[FORMERLY BLAKE'S,]
BONNET BLEACHERY
AND MANUFACTORY,
360½ WASHINGTON STREET, 360½
A few doors north of Essex St., over Tewksbury's Book Store.
BOSTON.
Every variety of Straw and Fancy Bonnets altered to fashionable shapes, cleansed and pressed in the very best manner. Also, Gentlemen's Summer Hats. Straw Bonnets Colored. Milliners furnished with Bonnet Blocks of the latest patterns.
Goods forwarded by Express, &c., will receive immediate attention.

Some voters support Senator Yancy Yakker because they like his ideas. Others are drawn to him because of his style and demeanor. A few even admit that his stature and southern drawl captivate them. Still others back him simply because he is a Democrat.

Topic Sentence:

....

....

....

....

Traffic in both directions came to a complete stop. People leaned from car windows to get a better look, adults smiling and children shrieking with delight. Even though the light regulating northbound traffic changed to green, no one moved or honked a horn.

Topic Sentence:

....

....

....

....

....

READING STRATEGIES LISTED

In the preceding activities, you have used the reading selections from real and simulated newspaper stories to enhance your students' reading skills. Though it is our goal as teachers to foster independent reading, we understand that Guided Reading is a step toward this goal. At right is a list of helpful strategies you have been using throughout the previous activities. As you proceed through the book, keep in mind that all of these can be used when you work with other sections of the newspaper.

FRONT PAGE SPRINGBOARD TO STUDENT MOTIVATION

In conclusion, you as a teacher can use a newspaper's front page as a springboard to motivate students to broaden their reading. As they follow the day's leading events on the inside pages, they will discover

GUIDED READING STRATEGIES

Work with students in small groups. You know from experience that some students "fall through the cracks" in large group settings. In small groups, such students feel less intimidated and more likely to participate in discussions and activities. Equally as important, you as a teacher can interact more effectively and devote additional time to those students who require it.

Preview the newspaper article that is to be read. Show students that they can learn to preview by reading headlines and picture captions and by skimming articles. More advanced readers can skim a story and quickly understand its content.

Ask questions and give directions designed to motivate and to arouse curiosity. Tell students to "look for" certain ideas and details in an article. Remind them to try to identify the "who, what, when, where, and why" often revealed in the lead paragraph of a story. Other questions that can be posed to stir imaginations and stimulate critical thinking include: "What would you have done?" "Have you ever been in a similar situation?" "How would you have solved the problem?" "Could the person in the story have reacted differently?" and so on.

Encourage students to make a list of new vocabulary words and to look up meanings in a dictionary. Remind them to try to discover the meaning of a word by its context.

other stories that will catch their eye and call for further investigation. To be in such a position to actually enjoy reading, however, students must be skillfully guided by the teacher through those steps designed to make them willing readers. This is especially true for those who have been struggling readers. These steps are based on scaffolding, which starts with what students know and builds from there.

CHAPTER THREE

The Editorial Page

EDITORIAL PAGE OFFERS WIDE RANGE OF ACTIVITIES

Few sections of a newspaper lend themselves to a wider range of student activities than the editorial page. Students can use this vital part of the daily newspaper to

• Distinguish between fact and opinion

• Read and interpret editorials and opinions

• Write editorials

• Compare their view with opinions expressed in editorials, in guest columns, and in letters to the editor

• Find meanings for new vocabulary words and use these words in sentences

• Identify various parts of speech in sentences

The editorial page is the "voice" of the paper—that is, it is a page on which the publisher and the editor can state the newspaper's position on important issues. Discuss with students why newspapers have editorial pages and what kinds of information are found on them. Discuss the concept of philosophy and explore how it might affect what appears on the editorial page.

The editorial pages also provide an important and popular public forum. Anyone can write letters to the editor to express an opinion on any matter of interest or controversy—from a dangerous intersection in the neighborhood to troop deployment in a foreign country.

The activities in this chapter can be done individually, in pairs or in groups. Make sure to have plenty of authentic editorial pages available to help students do the following: **The What and Why of the Masthead, What Is It?, Read and Interpret an Editorial, and Write an Editorial.**

• Before doing the rest of the activities, reproduce and distribute **What's on the Editorial Page** for student reference.

• Distribute samples of editorial pages for reference.

• Ask students to read about and identify at least one sample of each element.

• Have one or more students share findings with the whole class.

©2001 Rigby

What's on the Editorial Page

1. Masthead

The masthead is a box that lists the name, address, publisher, and editorial staff of the newspaper. The masthead also provides readers with the newspaper's telephone and e-mail addresses and information for submitting items to the paper. It may also include a statement of the publisher's philosophy.

2. Editorials

Editorials are unsigned articles that present the newspaper's official opinions on important issues. They are written by the paper's editorial board and, although they represent an opinion, they are based on facts. Editorials are designed to make readers think about issues. Some editorials explain, while others either persuade, criticize, or praise.

3. Columns

A column expresses the opinion of a single writer. Some columns are written by members of the newspaper's editorial staff. Others are syndicated—columns written by well known people—and are sold to a variety of newspapers. Columns contain the writer's name and often a picture of the writer. They cover a variety of subjects from serious to humorous.

4. Editorial Cartoons

Editorial pages often contain one or more political cartoons that focus on some important issue. The ability to interpret these cartoons requires knowledge of current events and issues portrayed in them.

5. Letters to the Editor

Readers of the newspaper are invited to express their opinions publicly by writing letters to the editor. This section is very popular with readers. These letters may be about local or national issues. They may be responses to articles or other letters that have appeared in the newspaper. People of all ages may write letters to the editor for publication in the paper. (Writers under 18 should have parental permission.) The letters must be signed and contain the writer's address and phone number for verification. The editorial staff decides which letters to publish. Letters containing threatening, obscene, or otherwise inappropriate material will not be published.

124 The Detroit News | Friday, January 5, 2001

1

The Detroit News

Founded August 23, 1873

MARK SILVERMAN
Publisher and Editor

EVERETT J. MITCHELL II
Managing Editor

NOLAN FINLEY
Editorial Page Editor

SUSAN BURZYNSKI
Associate Editor

LUTHER KEITH
Public Editor

Editorials represent the views of The Detroit News and are written by Nolan Finley, Jeffrey Hadden, Richard Burr, George Bullard, George Cantor, Shikha Dalmia, Bill Johnson, Diane Katz and Henry Payne

A GANNETT NEWSPAPER PUBLISHED DAILY, SATURDAY AND SUNDAY

CONGRESS SHALL MAKE *no law respecting an establishment of religion, or prohibiting the free exercise thereof, or abridging the freedom of speech, or of the press; or the right of the people peaceably to assemble, and to petition the Government for a redress of grievances.*

FIRST AMENDMENT TO THE CONSTITUTION

2

Don't Blame Deregulation

California is gripped by an energy crisis that threatens utility bankruptcies and widespread blackouts. The blame is largely being heaped on deregulation of the state's electricity supply, as if the free market has somehow gone haywire.

Far from it.

Had deregulation actually occurred in the Golden State, it's a safe bet that Gov. Gray Davis would not have unplugged all the Christmas lights. Rather, the state simply reconfigured the rules by which regulators control all the power — with predictably disastrous results.

Fortunately, Michigan's new utility restructuring plan avoids some of California's worst pitfalls. But to the extent that Lansing still governs the electrical grid, higher prices and supply shortages can result.

Twenty-four states have undertaken various forms of utility restructuring to introduce competition — and thus lower prices — in the power supply. None, however, have adopted so twisted a system as the one that was unanimously approved by the California Assembly in 1996.

Legislators there imposed price controls to "protect" consumers from utility price gouging. But California's investor-owned utilities have subsequently incurred some $7 billion in debt now that the power they must purchase on the open market costs 20 times more than the billing rate allowed by the state. Too, price controls have masked the market signals that otherwise would have tempered energy consumption as supplies grew scarce.

Contrary to the most basic principles of deregulation, California utilities were forced to divest all generating capacity and were prohibited from entering into stable long-term purchase contracts with power suppliers. Instead, the law requires that utilities buy electricity on the volatile spot market. Not surprisingly, prices have soared.

The state also required utilities to purchase "green power" from windmills and the like, which, according to the Los Angeles Times, cost $25 billion more than the same volume of conventional energy. And California's stringent environmental rules forced power generators to idle plants that prematurely hit emission limits in attempting to satisfy the surging demand.

The Issue

What lessons can be drawn from California's energy crisis?

Consumers turn up demand

Demand for electricity has risen nationwide. Electricity sales (billion kilowatt hours)

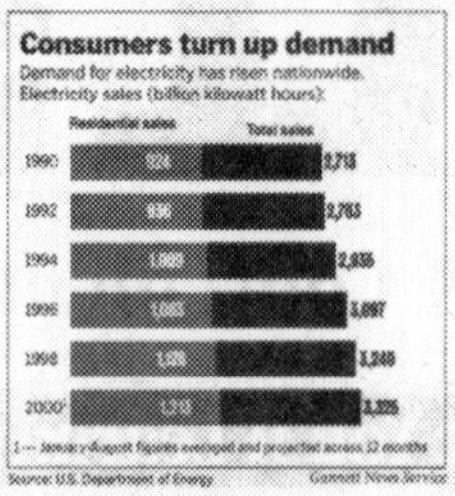

1 — January-August figures averaged and projected across 12 months

Source: U.S. Department of Energy — Gannett News Service

Indeed, environmental and other regulatory barriers have created a nationwide shortage of generating capacity. And unfounded fears about nuclear power has exacerbated the difficulties of siting and building power plants.

Michigan wisely rejected forced divestiture as well as the prohibitions on contracting adopted by California. But the Legislature has imposed price controls that will do more to inhibit than invite competition. A slew of other operating restrictions further impede the power industry just when conditions demand maximum operating flexibility.

Meanwhile, the U.S. Environmental Protection Agency has initiated a crackdown on Midwest utility emissions, thus steeply raising the costs of plant expansion and new construction.

It is unlikely that Michigan will be subject to the sorry predicament on the West Coast. Just how successful the state's restructuring will be remains to be seen. But regulators here would do well to heed California's hard-learned lesson: Government interference is no substitute for true competition.

New Court Chief: Steady Course

Maura Corrigan, who began her court career as a probation officer at Detroit's old Recorder's Court, is Michigan's 62nd chief justice. Ms. Corrigan was elected by her colleagues to a two-year term Thursday.

Under the Michigan Constitution, the state Supreme Court has the authority to administer all of the state's lower courts, so the chief justice has a strong platform for bringing about needed reforms. Chief Justice Corrigan told us that she is interested in building consensus among her colleagues on the Supreme Court for reforming the way justices are chosen.

Corrigan

After what she calls a "horrific campaign with a lot of name-calling" in which three of her colleagues were returned to the high court, Chief Justice Corrigan says one of her goals is to reassure the public that politics stops "at the courthouse door."

One way to do this, she told us, is to restore the public's confidence in the court by "showing confidence in each other." Ms. Corrigan says her administrative style would recognize that the court is made up of seven "co-equal" justices. She plans, she says, to consult with all of the justices and delegate tasks in the administration of the court system.

The court is divided, with five justices nominated by Republican Party state conventions and two justices nominated at Democratic Party conventions. And Chief Justice Corrigan, like the rest of the majority of her colleagues on the high court, has a particular philosophy in making rulings.

In an interview in the current edition of the Docket, a magazine for the alumni of the University of Detroit Mercy Law School, she termed her philosophy "interpretivist," which asks "what is the meaning of this particular provision as it was given to us," rather than seeking to impose her own views on the law.

While it is appropriate to discuss liberal and conservative philosophies in making decisions, Ms. Corrigan says, it is not appropriate to do so in the context of the administration of the justice system. The goal in administration, she adds, is to determine the most "just, economical and expeditious way to deliver court services to the public." And that goal, she says, is shared by all seven justices.

Chief Justice Corrigan says she and her colleagues would be "building on the work" of her predecessor, Elizabeth Weaver. Justice Weaver has already put forth a particular plan for moving from an elected to an appointed state Supreme Court — a goal we share. Chief Justice Corrigan proposes to seek internal support on the court and in the rest of the system for moving in the same direction.

In fact, that is a fair summary of the result of the high court's selection of a new chief justice: slightly different leadership style — same direction. That's good news for Michigan.

4

5

LETTERS

Keep the strife of Middle East out of schools

It saddens me greatly that there is a spillover of the Middle East conflict in our local neighborhood schools. ("Bloomfield schools probe ethnic incident," Jan. 4). It is my hope that the fifth graders' parents and the Bloomfield Hills school officials will be successful in their work in teaching that words do hurt and intolerance have no place in our community. But there is a lesson for us adults, too. We all need to take the responsibility to promote civil discourse and democratic values. We must all learn to live together with respect and tolerance. In our village, we must all use words carefully and sensitively. That is the American way.

SHARONA SHAPIRO
Michigan Area Director
American Jewish Committee
Bloomfield Hills

Heed fur protests

I am writing you in disgust that The News did not contact animal rights activists before running the recent fur article ("Brrrrrr! Turn to fur!," Dec. 8). I find it ironic that in an article discussing the ethics of wearing fur, The News only contacted the people who profit from the sale of it. It is a complete fallacy that people no longer protest fur. I've been to many fur protests this past year.

Fur production has to be the most brutal, bloody, ignominious industry in existence. Animals are killed by genital electrocution, gassing, trapping (which often takes several days) and sometimes even skinned alive.

Please write another article with both sides included in the argument.

MARK OSMOND
Goodrich

Barbaric industry

I am a 24-year-old student who knows lots of different people, and it is just common knowledge that wearing fur is barbaric, unevolved and disgusting. If The Detroit News thinks it's OK to use genital electrocution on small animals for a fashion statement, it is dead wrong. You know Jeff Dahmer was really into torturing animals before he moved on to people.

JEREMY JOHNSON-LEMIEUX
Milford

Warmth for selfish

After reading The News' terribly biased article glorifying the use of dead animals for their fur, I felt compelled to speak up for the animals and tell their side of the story.

In every case, a fur coat begins with tremendous violence and suffering, and ends with being draped across the backs of the vain and selfish. Animals who are trapped in our woods and streams — their natural homes — are subjected to torn muscles and tendons, as well as broken bones and lacerated skin. The favorite tool of the trapper is the steel-jaw leghold trap. This particular device is so barbaric it has been banned in many countries and several states. Sadly, Michigan is not among those.

Animals raised on so-called fur ranches suffer an even more horrendous fate. Since no laws regulate the slaughter of animals raised in these animal concentration camps, a "fur rancher" is free to kill them by any manner he deems suitable, and this is usually determined by what is simple and inexpensive.

The bottom line is that anyone selling or wearing fur — including the seemingly innocuous fur trim that plagues the fashion industry these days — is responsible for the suffering of a frightened creature, sentenced to a cruel and inhumane death only because her skin is more beautiful than our own. Be a compassionate consumer and shun the bloody fur trade.

LORI SAWYER
Warren

Inept Army buyers

[illegible] priorities" on President-elect George W. Bush's agenda, there is an old standby that has been looking for a solution during many administrations; blatant government waste and ineptitude. A case in point is a recent news report about people getting rich selling Army surplus back to the Army.

The Dec. 27 article ("U.S. pays top dollar for parts it sold cheap") even quotes a Harold Foote, from Merrimack, N.H., one of the business people involved in reselling the Army's stuff back to the Army, as saying: "The Defense Department is incompetent. The purchasing people don't stop buying, and the sales people don't stop selling."

After the $600 hammers and toilet seats that the United States was paying thousands of dollars for, one would think the government got the hint that it is being ripped off. But apparently that is not the case. It might not be the No. 1 priority of the new administration, but trying to stop such reckless waste and incompetence should be at least somewhere on the list of things that need "fixing."

STJEPAN BALOG
Warren

Priestly calling

One of the greatest Jesuit priests in American history, Fr. John Hardon, has been buried in Gesu Church in Detroit. Fr. Hardon stands out among nuns and priests for a soaring intellect that was matched by his humility and sacrifice.

He wrote 40 books, the most popular being — at more than 1 million sold — *The Catholic Catechism*, published by Doubleday. That thick reference work was a beacon of light in a decidedly confused post-Vatican II era that gave guidance to many Catholics, some of whom have gone on to the priesthood.

But the legacy of Fr. Hardon, who co-founded Call to Holiness, is not what he wrote, so much as what he lived. "Fr. Hardon had a great impact on the ordinary Catholic as well because of the embodiment of the very things he had been teaching, prayerfulness, devotion to the Blessed Sacrament, the participation in daily mass and his humility," said Fr. Eduard Perrone, pastor of Assumption Grotto Church in Detroit.

One of the remarkable things about him was that I never heard him say no to any request for his help. His life was one of continuous prayer, as I learned last year when he told me he had not seen a motion picture since the late 1960s.

"He made a promise early on in his Jesuit life that he would never take a vacation," Fr. Perrone said. And he never did.

JAY MCNALLY
Executive Director, Call to Holiness
Ann Arbor

Nonpartisan pardons

Recently President Bill Clinton pardoned some Democratic prisoners and [illegible] "last act" as president. However, there is a pattern here because in 1992, President George Bush issued Christmas Eve pardons to former Defense Secretary Caspar Weinberger and five others snared in the Reagan administration's Iran-contra scandal.

Is there a difference between the two so-called leaders?

ANDREW G. KATO
Flint

Speed up jackpots

I don't agree with the state of Michigan's suggestion that casinos did the Lotto in ("Casinos kill Lotto game," Dec. 21).

If you look at other states' lotteries, even our own Power Ball, the slow progression of growing pots is what made our Lotto game fail. Growing from $2 million to $2.5 million to $3 million, where others grow from $2 million to $4 million, $8 million, etc.

My co-workers still play the three- and four-digit games, almost to excess. They also drive to Ohio to get their lotto tickets. The bottom line is our Lotto wasn't progressive enough.

LARRY COURY
Ferndale

Find us!

detnews.com
http://detnews.com

Want to send The Detroit News a letter via E-mail? We can be reached at: **letters@detnews.com**

You can send us a fax at 313/222-6417. And we can still be reached the old-fashioned way, by mail, at 615 W. Lafayette Blvd., Detroit, MI 48226. Please include home and work phone numbers, plus city of residence. We want to hear from you.

3

Proposals provide hope to improve Detroit Police Department

BILL JOHNSON

The Detroit Police Department has a long history of unsolved and unresolved problems relating to police-community relations. The civilian Board of Police Commissioners, appointed by the mayor to serve as the public watchdog, also has a history of being ineffective. A citizen petition initiative, and an age-based police hiring proposal by a member of the City Council, may contain self-correcting measures.

Jonathan Kinloch heads an organization called Citizens for Police Accountability (CPA). The CPA was formed following revelations that Detroit led the nation in the number of citizens shot by police.

These officers, says Kinloch, have "basically created a me-against-them mentality." So, he says, the group decided to circulate petitions that would fundamentally change the structure of the police commission. The language reads in part: "Shall the City of Detroit Home Rule Charter be Amended to provide for a total of five (5) members of the board of police commissioners with (1) board member elected from each of five (5) districts..."

This initiative, Kinloch continues, is driven by a concern that the commission is a rubber stamp for the mayor. CPA members firmly believed, due to the increasing number of citizen complaints about the shootings and the internal operations of the police department, the commission would never be independent or representative as long as its members continued to be appointed.

"Right now, you have commissioners saying they don't know what's going on," he notes. "You have a report assessing the operations of the department that appears to have been suppressed. That should not be tolerated by a citizen panel whose sole responsibility is to keep the Police Department from running roughshod over the rights of the citizens it is sworn to protect."

The proposed elected commission would be under less pressure to bow to the wishes of the mayor than the current panel, Kinloch adds. "They also would be more accountable and responsible to the people."

If sufficient signatures are gathered and voters approve, a new commission would be elected from equally proportioned districts. This, according to the framers, is designed to foster greater accountability. Under the current system, it is impossible to target individual nonperforming commissioners. And they are answerable to no one but the mayor.

In a designated district, a commissioner would have a lot more incentive to see that cops are visible and responses are timely. If a specific district recorded an unusual amount of abuse complaints, residents would know whom to contact. Commissioners who were unable to meet public expectations would be subject to the wrath of voters.

On another front, Councilwoman Alberta Tinsley-Talabi has proposed to increase the hiring age for Detroit police officers from 18 to 21. Her push to amend the city's hiring practice is intended to "improve the overall quality and depth of officers entering the department."

"The authority, power and responsibility of a gun, badge and uniform can potentially outweigh a person who may have recently walked across a stage with a high school diploma or GED," Talabi stated in a press release. "I absolutely believe additional time spent obtaining at minimum of either an associate degree, three years consecutive work experience or three years military training would greatly assist in the further building of character, boosting confidence and increased maturity level of recruits."

She added: "The sensitivities and respect developed through life and personal experiences with diverse cultures are critical for for effective community policing and restoring public confidence in our Detroit Police Department."

Tinsley-Talabi concedes that raising the required age is not a panacea. She could not recall any case in which an 18-year-old officer was involved in a fatal shooting. However, she notes that what she has proposed is the accepted practice in New York City, Cleveland, Dallas, Las Vegas, Phoenix, Houston, New Orleans, Chicago and Los Angeles.

There is a growing public sentiment that the civilian Board of Police Commissioners ought to be independently empowered or eliminated. By almost any measure, the commission has been derelict in questioning or scrutinizing charges of police misbehavior. But since the commission serves at the pleasure of the mayor, the mayor ultimately bears the responsibility for its mismanagement. So why have a commission?

Certainly, no single charter amendment or age modification proposal could guarantee a cease-fire on Detroit citizens. A 10-member review panel selected by Police Chief Benny Napoleon to develop guidelines for the use of nonlethal force by his officers has no legal authority. The U.S. Justice Department inquiry into the use of fatal force by Detroit police officers will ultimately ride on the scope of the probe.

If efforts to restore public confidence are to be successful, everything must be on the table. To do nothing would be an even greater injustice.

Bill Johnson is a Detroit News editorial writer whose column is published on Friday. He can be reached at (313) 222-2299 or bjohnson@detnews.com.

The editorial page of *The Detroit News*, January 5, 2001.

1. Masthead

2. Editorials

3. Columns

4. Editorial Cartoons

5. Letters to the Editor

Name _____

The What and Why of the Masthead

In the space provided, create a masthead for an editorial page.

You may imitate one from an actual newspaper, or create one of your own.

SCOTLAND & IRELAND

an ever-changing pageant

Publisher

....

Editorial staff

....

Philosophy

....

....

....

....

....

Address of newspaper

....

....

....

Phone numbers and email information

....

....

....

Directions for submitting items to the paper

....

....

....

Name _____

What Is It?

You have learned that articles and letters that appear on the editorial page come from several sources. Some are written by editorial staff members and syndicated columnists. Others are written by the newspaper's readers.

• Read each description at right.

• Decide if the description fits an editorial, a letter to the editor, or a column; then label it on the line below it.

• Use **What's on the Editorial Page** for reference.

1. Susie B. of 210 Elm Street writes condemning her town's newspaper for advocating an increase in the property tax. Susie's contribution is an example of a(n):

....

....

2. Carlyle S., a member of the editorial staff of the *Baltimore Evening News,* identifies himself as the writer of an article charging citizens to get out and vote. Carlyle has written a(n):

....

....

3. John K. of 5543 Tall Pines Drive writes praising the *Hollow Herald* for its coverage of the recent Mud-Bogging Competition held at Lester Ledbetter's Mud-Bogging Track. John K. has written a(n):

....

....

4. The publisher of the *Chicago Chatter* writes an article revealing his newspaper's endorsement of Democrat Yancy Yakker for the U.S. Senate. This article is an example of a(n):

....

....

5. Nationally-known writer Philip T., whose work appears in newspapers across the country, writes an article giving his opinion on the United States selling weapons to East Snobovia. Philip's article is an example of a(n)

....

....

Name _____

Read and Interpret an Editorial

WHEN LAWS ARE UNJUST

By now I'm sure everyone in America has heard or read about the ordeal of Mary Diefenbaker. Her case illustrates that sometimes laws are unfair and need to be changed.

Mary was arrested a few days ago and released on bond until a date is set for her trial. Her crime? Violating a zoning ordinance by running an unauthorized animal shelter. Did she blatantly ignore the ordinance and proceed to commit the dastardly deed with which she is charged? Yes, but, in the opinion of this writer and probably the majority of people on this planet, with good reason.

In case you've been away for some time, Mary angered the authorities of Homerville by taking in 50 animals during Hurricane Wendy's recent trek up the coast. Frantic pet owners, aware that shelters and most motels do not allow animals of any kind, began calling Mary a few hours after orders went out to evacuate the barrier islands. They knew that Mary's farm is situated on high ground and her property would probably be safe during the storm. Would she please look after Fido? Or Rusty? Or Tom? Or Timmy Turtle? Or even Slithering Steve, everyone's favorite boa constrictor?

Mary, an incurable pet lover, could not refuse. With a large house, a barn, and a fenced-in farm, she certainly had room to take in an ark-full of animals. And she did! In a matter of a few hours, she became the happy host of some 20 dogs, 15 cats, 5 turtles, 3 hamsters, 4 white mice, and 3 snakes! Considering that all of these pets came from homes on the barrier islands, they would have surely perished from the winds and waves that wreaked havoc there. But at Mary's farm, they were safe, while their owners heard reports of their homes being swept out to sea.

You know the rest. As soon as the powers-that-be in Homerville got wind of Mary's charitable action, they cited her for running an animal shelter without a license. Now she faces a stiff fine—or worse—for acting as any concerned citizen might have acted.

Are some laws unjust? Are just and sensible laws sometimes interpreted unjustly? In the extraordinary case of Mary Diefenbaker, the answer is, "Yes."

Name _____

Read and Interpret an Editorial

Several years ago, a kind-hearted woman in New Jersey was actually arrested for taking in the animals of frantic pet-owners as they prepared to evacuate flooded areas of the state.

The editorial "When Laws are Unjust," although fictitious, is based on that event. Read it and answer the questions at right.

1. What is the main idea presented in the editorial?

....

2. What law did Mary Diefenbaker break?

....

3. Would you have done the same as Mary? Why or why not?

....

....

4. What would you do if you were ever forced to evacuate your home and you could not take your pets with you?

....

....

5. Do you agree with authorities that pets should not be allowed in public shelters? Why or why not?

....

....

6. Do people have the right to ignore laws they consider unjust? Why or why not?

....

....

....

7. Do you consider any rules at school unfair? If so, what is the proper way to go about changing them?

....

....

 Rigby Best Teachers Press

Name _____

Read and Interpret an Editorial

CHOOSE YOUR OWN EDITORIAL

Choose an editorial from the newspaper. Read it and answer the questions below.

1. What is the title of the editorial?

....

2. Identify the "who, what, where, when, and why" of the article.

W ....   **W** ....

W ....   **W** ....

W ....

3. What opinion does the writer express?

....

....

4. Was the editorial written to explain, persuade, criticize, or praise? Explain.

....

....

5. Do you agree or disagree with the opinion(s) of the writer? Why?

....

....

6. Did you find any unfamiliar vocabulary words in the editorial? Write them on the lines below. Can you guess the meanings from context? Write the definition for each on the lines below. If necessary, use the back of this sheet. Use a dictionary if necessary.

....

....

Name _____

Write an Editorial

Write an editorial on the lines at right.

You may write about an article from the newspaper, an issue in your school, or a local or national issue.

Remember, an editorial expresses an opinion, but is based on facts.

Rigby Best Teachers Press

THUNDERING
...the waterfalls in
YOSEMITE
NATIONAL PARK

COLUMNS AND LETTERS REVEAL INDIVIDUAL OPINIONS

Before doing the next group of activities, review with students that editorials represent official views of the newspaper as written by the editorial staff. Columns and letters to the editor, on the other hand, represent the opinions of individual writers and bear the writers' names.

Columns deal with a wide variety of subjects; they come in a variety of styles. Like editorials, some are meant to explain, persuade, criticize, or praise. Others are written only to entertain. The latter usually appear under the same title, be it a sewing column entitled "Here's Needling You" or a humorous column called "Frolicking With Franconi." Columns may appear on pages other than the editorial page. The sports, business, and community affairs sections are just three places of the newspaper that might feature columns.

The activities that follow focus on columns, letters to the editor, and political cartoons. The **Read and Interpret a Column** activities and the **Interpret a Letter to the Editor** activities provide opportunities to examine these elements of the editorial page. Finally, **Review of the Editorial Page** provides an opportunity for students to review what they have learned about the editorial section of the newspaper.

Name _____

Read and Interpret a Column

A MATTER OF VALUES

BY VICTOR McFADDEN

Yesterday I noticed that Speedy Hinson, swivel-hipped running back of the New York Whales, had signed a 3-year extension to his contract that guarantees him a sweet $2.5 million a year. Speedy stated that the pay raise merely compensates him for his value to the team, his fans, and to America as a whole.

Along similar lines, I read a few weeks ago in *Wow Magazine* that Ginger Gorgeous, who starred recently in the blockbuster movie *Tinsel Town Romance*, was rewarded for her hard work with a new contract by Colossal Studios. How do you like that, Speedy! You have to play football for about 4 months each year to collect your 2.5 million; Ginger will receive that and more for each picture she makes. Ginger's comment to the press was,

considering her value to the entertainment world, she is worth that—and more!

Pardon me while I get sick! Since when are sports heroes and film stars worth these outrageous sums? Sure, I've heard it argued that they contribute more than most people to the economy, that their careers are short compared to other workers, that their endeavors provide hard-working Americans with much-needed entertainment as an outlet for their worries and emotions, and so on and so on.

My response to both Speedy and Ginger is this: if your contributions are so vital to America's well being, then what about those made by such unsung heroes as teachers, police officers, fire fighters, and others like them? Just how valuable are the services provided by these dedi-

cated public servants? Does $30,000 a year adequately compensate a teacher for his or her efforts to mold character and responsibility in our children? Is $28,000 annually enough to offset the many times that police officers ensure our safety? And what about the pitiful sum paid to our fire fighters who, in recent years of drought, have spent more time fighting forest fires than they have at home with their children? Are the services performed by these public employees less important than those provided by athletes and actors?

This writer maintains that as Americans we need to take a close look at our values. If an athlete or performer is worth millions a year, what value can we place on people whose work affects our safety and our education?

The Editorial Page

Name _____

Read and Interpret a Column

How well do you remember what you have just read?

- Without looking back over the column "A Matter of Values," see how many of the questions you can answer correctly.

- After you have answered as many questions as you can from memory, go back and skim the column for the answers to the others.

REMEMBERING "A MATTER OF VALUES"

1. What is the name of the running back referred to in the column? For which team does he play?

   ....

2. How many year's extension was the running back given on his present contract?

   ....

   ....

3. With which studio did Ginger Gorgeous sign a new contract? How much will she earn for each picture?

   ....

   ....

4. What is the name of the magazine that ran the story about Ms. Gorgeous's contract?

   ....

   ....

5. What figure does the writer use as the average salary for a teacher?

   ....

   For a police officer?

   ....

Name _____

Read and Interpret a Column

THINKING ABOUT "A MATTER OF VALUES"

- Read "A Matter of Values," a fictitious example of a guest column that might appear in your local paper.

- Refer to the column to answer the questions on the next page.

1. What is the writer's opinion about salaries?

....

....

2. Do you agree with the writer's opinions? Why or why not?

....

....

....

3. What, in your opinion, are reasonable salaries for professional athletes? For actors? Explain.

....

....

....

....

4. Do you think teachers, police officers, and firefighters earn enough money for the jobs they do? Explain.

....

....

....

....

Name _____

Read and Interpret a Column

CHOOSE YOUR OWN COLUMN

Choose a column from the editorial page of a recent newspaper. Read the column and answer the questions below. Attach the column to this sheet.

OPTIONAL ACTIVITY: Write your own column. The subject can be humorous or serious. Prepare display copies with your photograph.

1. What is the title of the column? Who wrote it?

....

2. What is the main idea the writer presents?

....

3. Does the column explain, persuade, criticize, praise, or entertain? Explain.

....

....

4. Do you agree with the writer's viewpoint? Explain.

....

5. List all proper nouns used by the writer in the column.

....

....

6. Did you find any unfamiliar vocabulary words in the column? Write them on the lines below. Can you guess the meanings from context? Write the definition for each on the lines below. Use a dictionary if necessary.

....

....

FREEDOM OF SPEECH GUARANTEED BY CONSTITUTION

Look for the man who runs the "RED CROWN" PUMP

Before moving on to the activities for letters to the editor, review with students the purpose for and characteristics of editorials and columns. Discuss the concept of freedom of speech and the editorial page as a public forum in a democracy. Newspapers fought for and won this same right as a result of the famous Zenger trial in 1735; in 1791 it became a constitutional right guaranteed in the Bill of Rights. It naturally followed that newspapers should grant this same privilege to their readers.

Remind students that the letters to the editor section of the editorial page serves as a forum for different points of view. It is democracy in action.

PUBLIC STENOGRAPHER

CONFECTIONER.

British officials burn John Peter Zenger's *New York Weekly Journal,* November 6, 1734.

©2001 Rigby

Name _____

Interpret a Letter to the Editor

ABOUT OLD GLORY

Yesterday I was saddened and dismayed at the lack of patriotism shown by many people who stood with me and watched our annual Independence Day parade. It's not that they committed any obvious acts that could be interpreted as unpatriotic or disruptive. They did not jeer or hoot or anything like that. In fact, it's not what they did that bothers me; it's what they didn't do. What they didn't do was show proper respect for our flag.

Whatever happened to the days when people respectfully held their hand over their hearts, or took off their hats, or stood at attention, or—in the case of a few—even saluted as Old Glory passed by? As I looked around, I saw several elderly people standing as if they were saying "The Pledge of Allegiance" and one or two others standing at attention. But, sad to say,

that was about it. In the eyes of everyone else, the American flag passing by was no different from the flags carried by the twirlers of our local high school band.

"Big Deal!" you might say. "What's the big deal about the flag? After all, it's only a *thing*! A piece of cloth waving at the end of a stick! What does that have to do with patriotism?"

Well, dear reader, let me remind you that thousands of Americans have died defending that *thing*. Even

during colonial days, others fought and died to assure that what that *thing* stood for would become a reality. That *thing* represents everything this nation stands for, and any American who doesn't understand or appreciate that fact needs to re-enroll in American History 101!

As American citizens, we, as a matter of course, should always show respect for our flag. Otherwise, we are not worthy of all the rights and freedoms associated with it.

William Rolfe

Name _____

Interpret a Letter to the Editor

"ABOUT OLD GLORY"

1. What is the main idea expressed in the letter?

....

....

2. Do you agree with the writer? Why or why not?

....

....

....

3. Which statements made by the writer are opinions? Which are facts? List them on the lines below.

Opinions:

....

....

Facts:

....

....

5. What does the word *patriotism* mean to you? Explain your answer by writing a paragraph on the lines below. If necessary, use the back of this sheet.

....

....

....

....

....

Name _____

Interpret a Letter to the Editor

CHOOSE YOUR OWN LETTER

Choose a letter to the editor from the editorial page of the newspaper. Read it and respond to the questions below. Attach the letter to this sheet.

1. Who wrote the letter?

....

2. What is the main idea of the letter?

....

3. Do you agree with the writer? Why or why not?

....

4. Was the letter written to explain, persuade, praise, or criticize? Explain.

....

5. Do you think the writer's letter is based on facts? Explain.

....

....

6. Do you think the writer of the letter is likely to get a response from another reader? Why or why not?

....

....

7. Did you find any unfamiliar vocabulary words in the editorial? Write them on the lines below. Can you guess the meanings from context? Write the definition for each on the lines below. Use a dictionary if necessary.

....

....

CARTOONS CONVEY MESSAGE QUICKLY, EFFECTIVELY

In the case of political cartoons, the old saying "a picture is worth a thousand words" certainly holds true. A cartoon will often catch the attention of a reader much faster than a headline and its accompanying article. It can convey a message quickly and effectively.

Political cartoons can present a challenge for the reader. Comprehension depends on familiarity with the various symbols and caricatures used. For example, at the national level, cartoonists use such symbols as the donkey to represent the Democratic Party and the elephant for the Republican Party. At the international level, the bear, for example, was synonymous with the former Soviet Union and Uncle Sam with the United States.

Caricature—sketches that exaggerate a person's peculiarities—is used to depict people in the cartoons. Presidents and other leaders are frequent subjects. Abraham Lincoln was always sketched with large ears (which he certainly had); so was Ross Perot, a 1990s presidential candidate on the Reform Party ticket. Richard Nixon was drawn with a ski nose, Bill Clinton with a pudgy, cherubic face. And so it goes.

The **Interpret a Political Cartoon** activity on the following page will give your students the opportunity to explore "Join, or Die," the first political cartoon ever to appear in America. **Interpret a Political Cartoon, Choose Your Own Cartoon** gives them the opportunity to analyze an actual cartoon from the newspaper. **Review of the**

Editorial Page provides a review of what students have learned about the editorial page.

• Distribute copies of **Interpret a Political Cartoon, Join or Die**.

• Explore students' knowledge of the cartoon's historical context—pre-Revolutionary America.

• Have students work individually, in pairs, or in groups to complete the questions.

• Share interpretations with the class.

A political cartoon from the 1930s critical of President Roosevelt's New Deal.

©2001 Rigby

Name _____

Interpret a Political Cartoon

"Join, or Die" was the first political cartoon to appear in America. It was printed in Benjamin Franklin's *The Pennsylvania Gazette* on May 9, 1754, and was reprinted in newspapers throughout the colonies. It reappeared more than twenty years later when the Revolutionary War began.

Study the cartoon and answer the questions at the bottom of the page.

JOIN, or DIE.

1. What was the main idea Benjamin Franklin was trying to convey with his cartoon?

....

....

....

2. Why do you think Franklin presented the snake as disjointed—in broken segments?

....

....

....

3. What did Franklin's cartoon tell about the American colonies in 1754 when it was first published? What did it tell about the colonies during the Revolutionary period?

....

....

....

Name _____

Interpret a Political Cartoon

CHOOSE YOUR OWN CARTOON

Choose a political cartoon from the editorial page of a newspaper. Refer to the cartoon as you answer the questions below. Attach the cartoon to this sheet.

1. Are there caricatures in the cartoon? If yes, who do they represent?

....

2. Are there special symbols in the cartoon? If yes, what do they stand for?

....

3. What is happening in the cartoon?

....

....

....

4. What opinion is the cartoonist trying to get across?

....

....

....

5. Do you agree with the cartoonist's opinion? Why or why not?

....

....

....

6. Can you find the name of the cartoonist? If so, write it on the line below.

....

Name _____

Review of the Editorial Page

Use what you have learned about the editorial page to answer the questions below.

1. How does an editorial differ from a column?

   ....

   ....

   ....

2. Does the newspaper have to publish all letters to the editor sent by readers? If not, what kind of letter might not be published?

   ....

   ....

   ....

3. Why are editorial cartoons effective ways to influence opinion?

   ....

   ....

   ....

4. Do editorials, columns, and letters to the editor contain facts? Explain.

   ....

   ....

   ....

5. While reading an editorial or column, what should you do when you encounter words and terms you do not understand? Why?

   ....

   ....

   ....

CHAPTER FOUR

Local and State News

LOCAL NEWS REALLY HITS HOME

While national and international news is important and may dominate the front page, local, and regional stories are, in fact, often more interesting to readers. Information contained in local stories may have a closer connection and more immediate impact than stories of faraway places and events. Local news covers counties, towns or cities, or neighborhoods and is often populated by familiar people, places, and events.

As in the case of local news, readers often feel more connected to news that focuses on the home state. Some stories cover state politics and laws; others are quick to catch the eye of the reader because of an interesting event. This Florida occurrence is a case in point to be shared with students.

Remind students that the purpose of news is to inform. Unlike editorials and columns, state and local news stories will contain facts, not opinions.

• Write the following headlines on the board: **Ladies Hijack Helicopter for Prison Escape** and **Out-of-Gas Getaway**.

• Ask, "Who would be interested in reading a news story about this?" Read aloud the descriptions on page 59.

• Ask students what conclusions they can draw from these stories.

• Ask students to share any similar stories they remember from the newspaper or other news source.

The Local News section of *The Detroit Free Press*, January 5, 2001.

©2001 Rigby

LADIES HIJACK HELICOPTER FOR PRISON ESCAPE

Two determined women hijacked a helicopter at a local airport and forced the pilot at gunpoint to fly to the nearby state prison, where they supposedly had plans to aid in a prison escape. Just before reaching the site near the prison, the pilot convinced the women of the wisdom of turning back because of inclement weather. He returned the craft to the small airport where it had been commandeered. The women left the scene in a stolen car but were soon stopped and taken into custody by law enforcement officials. The pilot was shaken but unharmed.

OUT-OF-GAS GETAWAY

An amateur bank robber held up a regional bank at a shopping mall. Seated in the get-away car with the engine running was his accomplice. After running from the bank with an undisclosed amount of cash, the robber jumped into the get-away car, which sped off in a cloud of dust. But wait! The escape vehicle, after burning *rubber and giving stun-*ned bystanders the impression that it was off to the races, came to an abrupt stop at a gas station just across the parking lot! While they were in the process of getting gas, the local police showed up and carted them off to jail.

SEE THE HISTORY OF **BRITAIN**

LOCAL NEWS SPARKS INTEREST AMONG RELUCTANT READERS

Local and state sections of their newspapers are full of such stories. Such stories would probably pique the curiosity of even the most reluctant readers. After all, how often are helicopters hijacked for the purpose of busting someone out of prison? And how often are the hijackers women? Don't prison escapes evoke an action movie sort of excitement?

The bank robbery escape story might be appropriately titled "The World's Dumbest Crooks."

While not all state and local stories are of this ilk, there are numerous local stories that will captivate and hopefully motivate your students to read. And a funny thing happens when students are reading something that catches their interest: their reading skills unwittingly improve. They see how words, sentences, and paragraphs come together to tell a story. They are introduced to new vocabulary, new concepts, new places, and new people.

ROOFING

LOCAL NEWS OFFERS MANY TEACHING OPTIONS

• Clip samples of local and/or state news stories to distribute to students. Be sure to include some articles about unusual happenings.

• Also ask students to bring in any interesting local and/or state stories they find. Encourage them to look for stories that include people and places familiar to them. Remember to preview them before including them in the group to be shared with the class.

• Have students complete the reproducible **Examining a Local or State News Story** individually, in pairs, or in groups. Provide support as needed for drawing conclusions.

• Have students share selected stories with the class.

• Ask students to write their vocabulary words from **Examining a Local or State News Story** on the board or on an overhead.

• Have students complete the **Share New Vocabulary Words** reproducible.

• Have students write a local news story based on a happening in the school or community using the **Write an Article About a Local Happening** reproducible.

OPTIONAL ACTIVITY:
Hold a "contest" to see who can bring in the most unusual news story. Select the top three and have students share them with the class. Post all appropriate entries in the room.

OPTIONAL ACTIVITY:
Submit selected student articles to the local newspaper. Obtain the necessary student and parental permission for submissions.

Name _____

Examining a Local or State News Story

Read the first paragraph of an article of state or local news. Answer questions 1 and 2 below, finish reading the article, and answer the rest of the questions. Reference a state or local map to answer questions. Attach the article to this sheet.

1. What is the headline on the article?

....

2. According to the first paragraph, what is the article about?

....

3. In what city(s) or community did the story(ies) take place? ....

4. What road, if any, is closest to the location of the story? ....

5. How far is the location of this story from your city or community? ....

6. Write a brief summary of the article.

....

7. Write two alternate headlines that could replace the one that was used.

....

8. What is your opinion about the events in the article?

....

9. What conclusion can you draw from reading this article?

....

10. Did you find any unfamiliar vocabulary words in the story? Write them on the lines below. Can you guess the meanings from context? Write the definition for each on the lines below. Use a dictionary if necessary. If necessary, use the back of this sheet.

....

....

Name _____

Share New Vocabulary Words

Copy the vocabulary words shared by the other students in your class. Write the definition for each word. Use a dictionary to help. Choose five of the words and use them in sentences. You may use more than one word in a sentence; you do not have to have five sentences. Use the back of the paper if you need more space.

Word

Definition

©2001 Rigby

Name _____

Write an Article About a Local Happening

Pretend you are a reporter for your local newspaper. Write an article about a recent event or happening in your school or community on the lines below.

Remember to answer the 5 Ws: *Who, What, Where, When, Why?*

Use the back of the paper if you need additional space.

Be sure to give your article an appropriate headline.

Ask your teacher or someone in your family if you need help choosing a subject.

Headline: _____

_____

_____

_____

_____

_____

_____

_____

_____

_____

_____

_____

_____

_____

PREFIXES USED IN WORD ATTACK STRATEGY

The last two activities in this chapter provide practice in finding definitions through prefixes—a helpful word attack skill.

• Review with students the definition of prefix.

• Write a few prefixes on the board and ask students to list words that begin with them. Ask, "How does the prefix help you understand the meaning of the word?"

• Have students search state and local news articles to find words with the prefixes listed on **Know Your Prefixes** and **Use Prefixes in Words**.

• Have students work individually, in pairs, or in groups.

Era Works, Atlantic Docks, Brooklyn.

MANUFACTORY OF

GWYNNE'S PUMPING ENGINE,

"*The Voyage of Your Dreams*"

AROUND the WORLD

London

Paris

Berlin

Name _____

Know Your Prefixes

A prefix is a word part that is added to the beginning of another word or word part to make a new word. If you know the meanings of the most common prefixes, you can often figure out the meaning of the word in which you find it.

Do the following for each of the eighteen common prefixes listed below:

- Write the definition. Use a dictionary if you need help.

- For each prefix, try to find one or more words that use it in an article about state or local news.

- Write the words found on the lines after the appropriate prefixes.

1. auto _____

2. mal _____

3. mis _____

4. mono _____

5. poly _____

6. pre _____

7. trans _____

8. re _____

9. sub _____

10. semi _____

11. im _____

12. intra _____

13. intro _____

14. ir _____

15. hypo _____

16. bene _____

17. con _____

18. inter _____

Name _____

Use Prefixes in Words

Write a word for each prefix listed below. You may use words that you found in an article about state or local news, or words you found in the dictionary.
    Write a sentence with each word.

Prefix	Word
1. auto	
2. inter	
3. dys	
4. con	
5. mis	
6. hypo	
7. mono	
8. intra	
9. pre	
10. sub	

CHAPTER FIVE

The National Scene

NATIONAL NEWS REACHES STUDENTS FIRST

It is possible that your students are more aware of what is taking place on the national level than locally. Families who discuss the news together may be more likely to discuss what is going on in Congress and the White House than in a local official's campaign to get the road leading to his property paved. That voter turnout is usually greater when national offices are on the ballot would seem to indicate a higher level of interest in national matters. Many television news programs focus heavily on national news, and these programs often provide a major source of news for busy families.

In classrooms where both teachers and students may be transplants from a variety of states—even countries—national news can provide a more common frame of reference for discussion.

POLITICS SUBJECT OF NATIONAL COVERAGE

Given our democratic form of government, it is no surprise that political news features very prominently in the national news. However, it is important for students to understand that national news encompasses more than just the actions of the president and the national government. Anything that happens out-

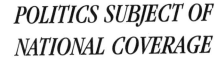

The Nation section of *The Detroit News*, January 5, 2001.

side of the home state is national news. This includes everything from natural disasters to famous personalities and their latest antics. Sandwiched between these are stories about—among other things —crime, strikes, personal heroics, the stock market, and sometimes demonstrations. In addition, national news often covers America's relationship with other countries, thereby adding elements of international news to the mix.

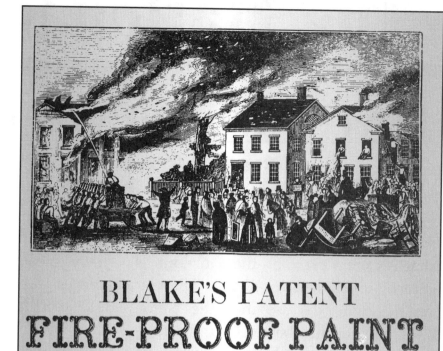

BLAKE'S PATENT
FIRE-PROOF PAINT

KEY VOCABULARY WORDS IDENTIFIED

Because so much of what happens nationally involves Congress, the White House, and foreign policy and relations, certain vocabulary is typical to articles covering national news. On the next page is a list of terms often encountered in these articles. It is by no means comprehensive; consider it a start. The list also contains lines for you and your students to add others.

You may choose from a variety of ways to help students become familiar with the terms. Years of classroom experience taught me that students often enjoy learning when it involves a game. A few suggestions for easy games follow the list of common terms. You can adapt almost any sport or, if you prefer a non-competitive venue, form cooperate groups and share findings.

Name _____

Commonly Used Terms from the National News

Use the lines to add other terms you find as you read national news stories.

PEOPLE

ambassador	attorney general	diplomat
electorate	prime minister	premier
pressure group	GOP	minority
Speaker of the House	bureaucracy	labor

....

....

PLACES

Capitol Hill	embassy	Oval Office
	Wall Street	

....

....

THINGS AND ACTIONS

arbitration	alliance	bill
campaign	capital	caucus
censure	deficit	filibuster
gun control	impeachment	inflation
issue	national debt	primary
recession	referendum	revenue
term	tariff	welfare

....

....

....

GAMES SUGGESTED FOR LEARNING COMMON TERMS

For all games and activities, you may choose a variety of ways to give a correct response. Students may be asked to:

• give a definition of the term from a dictionary or glossary

• locate the term in the context of a newspaper article and to read aloud the sentence in which it appears

• use the term in an original sentence that reflects an understanding of the definition

• state the appropriate term when a definition is given.

Baseball:
Divide the class into two teams.

• Students take turns answering questions when their team is "at bat."

• Award a base hit for each correct answer.

• Call a strike for each incorrect answer.

• Change at-bat teams after 1 or 3 outs.

Basketball:
Divide the class into two teams.

• Award a basket for each correct answer.

• After one team makes a basket, the other "gets the ball."

• Call a turnover for each incorrect answer.

Cooperative Groups:
Divide the class into several groups.

• Assign each group a number of the terms.

• Specify a time allotment for finding the terms in newspaper articles or for finding the definitions of the terms.

• Have each group share results with the whole group.

> **OPTIONAL ACTIVITY:**
> Have the students create a game for learning the common terms.

Dreams Come True in "Isle of June"

FAMOUS CRUISES

Nassau
Bahamas
"Isle of June"

STORE

SIGNS

NEWS ACTIVITIES PROVIDE OPPORTUNITY FOR COMPREHENSION, CRITICAL THINKING

Once the students have a working knowledge of the commonly used terms, proceed to the remaining activities in this chapter.

The following activities provide an opportunity for students to demonstrate comprehension and critical thinking skills using a national news story. They include **Examining a National News Article** activities, **Fact and Opinion, Read and Comment on a National News Story, Name those Synonyms in the National News,** and **Write an Editorial Based on a News Story**.

Many of the activities suggested in previous chapters can be easily adapted for use with reading selections covering national news. Students can, for example, use national news selections to do the following:

• identify topic sentences and main ideas

• answer questions about the content of a national news story

• look up meanings of unfamiliar words and use the words in sentences

• identify various parts of speech in selected paragraphs of a story

• use prefixes to help in comprehending the meanings of new words—to name a few.

All the while, you can work with them individually and/or in groups using the various guided reading strategies mentioned on page 35.

> *OPTIONAL ACTIVITY:*
> Ask students to brainstorm issues that currently dominate the national news and list them on the board. Have each student choose one on which to write a one- or two-page essay using current news articles and other references. Students should include the following in their essays:
> 1. a factual introduction to the issue
> 2. personal opinion on the issue
> 3. suggestion for resolving the issue

Name _____

Examining a National News Article

The following fictitious article is similar to many others that have appeared in newspapers nationwide in recent years. Violence in schools across the country has focused national attention on the issue of stricter regulations of firearms, particularly of those commonly referred to as "assault weapons."

DEBATE CONTINUES ON GUN CONTROL

Washington (WP)—In what has become an annual ritual since the rash of school shootings that shocked and sickened our nation, Congress will begin debate next week on the issue of gun control. Americans in support of a measure to ban automatic and semi-automatic weapons say they hope that this time Congressional leaders will fulfill their responsibility and call for new and stronger gun control legislation. Opponents of more regulation maintain we need stricter enforcement of existing laws—not new and more restrictive laws.

For the most part, opinion on Capitol Hill is divided along party lines. Republicans, in general, have traditionally fought

Sen. Robert Toricelli, a New Jersey Democrat, left, is shown some police weapons. Toricelli said he will introduce two important pieces of gun legislation.

©2001 Rigby

Examining a National News Article

past attempts to strengthen gun laws, while most Democrats have supported such efforts. Republicans continue to cite the Second Amendment, which states: *A well-regulated militia, being necessary to the security of a free state, the right of the people to keep and bear Arms shall not be infringed.* Democrats counter that the right to bear arms does not include the freedom to own assault weapons. Their only purpose—they remind their Republican counterparts—is to kill people in mass numbers.

Democrats also assert that Republicans are against gun control because of the large contributions they receive from the National Rifle Association. Republicans readily admit that they do receive contributions from the NRA, but they insist this has not influenced their opinions on gun control. A number of Republicans further main-

tain that "Guns do not kill people; people kill people."

Republican Senator Throckmorton Sims, interviewed last night with Democratic Congresswoman Josephine Trilling on *Face the People*, stated, "No amount of gun control is going to prevent criminals and others bent on violence from getting their hands on guns. Real gun control begins at home through proper education. Parents have an obligation to instruct their children in gun safety and the proper use of guns."

"That's highly idealistic," countered Congresswoman Trilling, co-sponsor of the bill to ban automatic and semi-automatic weapons. "It's like saying we don't need traffic laws because parents and driving schools teach the rules of the road and drivers' safety. It is absurd."

Just as Sims, who leads the opposition to the bill,

and Trilling could not reach an agreement on *Face the People*, Congress is expected to debate the issue for weeks and is unlikely to reach an agreement or pass the bill.

CAP HAITIEN
CARTAGENA
CURACAO
SAN JUAN
ST. PIERRE
BARBADOS
PORT OF SPAIN
LA GUAYRA
NASSAU
ST. THOMAS
SANTO DOMINGO
PORT AU PRINCE
FORT DE FRANCE
HAVANA

Name _____

Examining a National News Article

Read the article "Debate Continues on Gun Control." Answer the questions at right.

Better Vision

1. What is the main idea of the article?

....

....

....

2. According to the article, what position do many Republicans hold on gun control?

What position do the Democrats hold?

....

....

....

....

3. Which amendment do opponents of gun control cite to support their position?

....

4. Do you think there should be more or less laws to regulate the manufacture and sale of guns? Why do you feel as you do?

....

....

....

....

....

....

Name _____

Fact and Opinion

Read each statement at right and decide whether the statement is fact or opinion.

Write **F** in front of each statement of fact and **O** in front of each opinion.

Remember that a fact is something that can be proven, while an opinion is simply what someone thinks.

Reference the article "Debate Continues on Gun Control."

_____ 1. Gun control is an important issue in the minds of many Americans today.

_____ 2. As a law-abiding citizen, a person should have the right to purchase any kind of gun he or she desires.

_____ 3. Guns do not kill people; people do.

_____ 4. Owning a gun does not mean that a person supports the position of the National Rifle Association on gun control.

_____ 5. All Democrats favor stronger regulations on the sale of firearms.

_____ 6. All Republicans are against gun control.

_____ 7. Even the strongest of laws would probably not prevent criminals from getting their hands on guns.

_____ 8. No person under the age of 18 should be allowed to own a gun of any kind.

_____ 9. The use of a gun in such an activity as hunting is dangerous without proper instruction in handling and safety.

_____ 10. People who desire to own a lot of guns will probably commit crimes with them.

The Second Amendment to the United States Constitution states, "A well-regulated militia, being necessary to the security of a free state, the right of the people to keep and bear Arms shall not be infringed."

What do you think this amendment means? Compare your opinion with those of your classmates.

....

....

....

....

Name _____

Read and Comment on a National News Story

Select and read a national news article on a subject other than the national government. Then refer to the article to answer the questions below.

Attach your article to this sheet.

1. Write the headline for the article you read.

....

2. Write an alternate headline for the article you read.

....

2. What is the main idea presented in the article?

....

3. Where did the article take place? In which direction would you travel from where you live to get there?

....

4. What people and/or organizations were important in this article?

....

5. Write a brief summary of the article on the lines provided.

....

....

....

6. Did you find any unfamiliar vocabulary words in the story? Write them on the lines below. Can you guess the meanings from context? Write the definition for each on the lines below. Use a dictionary if necessary.

....

....

Name _____

Name Those Synonyms from the National Scene

Select and read a national news article.

Identify five verbs and five adjectives used in the article and write them on the lines below.

Write one synonym for each of the verbs and adjectives that you have selected.

Use a dictionary or thesaurus as needed.

Verb	**Synonym**
....	....
....	....
....	....
....	....

Adjective	**Synonym**
....	....
....	....
....	....
....	....

Choose three of the verbs and three of the adjectives selected and use them in sentences on the lines below. Use the back of this sheet or a separate sheet of paper if you need more room.

....

....

....

....

....

Name _____

Write an Editorial Based on a News Story

Imagine you are the editor of a newspaper.

    Select and read a national news article.

    Write an editorial based on the information in this article.

    Write a headline for your editorial.

    Remember that an editorial written by a staff member expresses the official opinion of the newspaper.

Headline

....

....

....

....

....

....

....

....

....

....

....

....

....

....

....

....

....

World News

TECHNOLOGY BRINGS WORLD NEWS TO FINGERTIPS

A song popular many years ago began,

Far away places with strange-sounding names,

Far away over the sea,

If far away places had strange-sounding names 50 years ago, take a glance at a modern map today. Timor? Sri Lanka? Chechnya? Kosovo? Rwanda? Bosnia-Herzegovina? These are but a few "hot spots" in the world that have captured headlines in the daily news in recent years. Remember Grenada? Guyana? Uganda? Zimbabwe?

Modern technology places—virtually at our fingertips—the tools to bring up-to-the-minute news of the world into our homes. At the click of a remote control or by a log-on and a few keystrokes, we can read reports and view images related to current events in the most remote corners of the planet. Countries and leaders with exotic-sounding names become household words as we visit them via the daily news reports.

By the time students have reached the intermedi-ate grades, they have most likely been exposed—either at home, school, or both—to current international events. They may already be familiar with such terms as global economy and know what OPEC does or does not do to affect oil and gasoline prices from Albuquerque to Timbuktu.

Reading about world news can provide a rich inter-disciplinary experience for students. International news cannot escape being a history and/or geography lesson and often a math lesson.

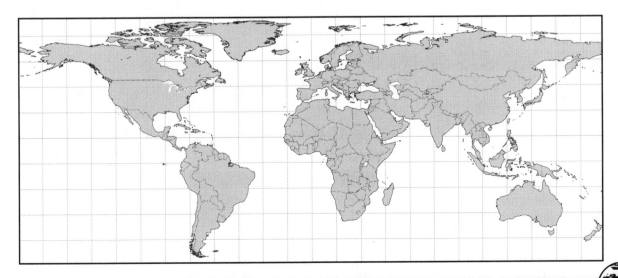

CONSTANTLY CHANGING WORLD CHALLENGES TEACHERS, STUDENTS

A geography lesson is inherent in an examination of world news events. For example, before our textbooks and maps could reflect the changes, we learned of Yugoslavia's dramatic regional realignments from the media. News reports in the 1990s turned our attention to Kosovo and Serbia. Once there were East and West Germanys. Where there was a Soviet Union, there are now many countries. The country of Israel was established as a modern nation rather recently—in 1948—compared to its centuries of history.

In this ever-changing world, it is a daunting task to keep up with the latest information on world events and political borders. Fortunately, there are a number of resources to help us. Radio and television news and daily newspapers are good sources of information about what is happening throughout the world. *The World Almanac and Book of Facts, New York Times Almanac,* and *the Time Almanac*—all updated yearly—are excellent quick resources that can be referenced in a library or purchased for a nominal price.

You can also get information about geography and history by consulting two excellent Internet sites. **www.yahooligans.com** is student- and teacher-friendly. Click on Social Studies under the School Bell heading or on Around the World. The CIA website at **www.odci.gov/cia/publications/factbook** also allows you to access information about countries around the world.

Remember to use where appropriate the Guided Reading Strategies found in Chapter 2 on page 35.

As in the chapter on national news, a list of **Commonly Used Terms from the International News** is offered on page 81. You can probably think of others, as well as a variety of ways to introduce them to your students. In addition, several activities follow that provide students with an opportunity to become even more acquainted with the terminology listed.

Once your students have gained a better understanding of the Commonly Used Terms and have completed the activities connected with them, other activities follow that test their comprehension of several articles dealing with international news.

DISCOVER AMERICA'S OWN *tropical paradise* HAWAII

Name _____

Commonly Used Terms from the International News

aggression	emigrant	immigration	sanctions
balance of power	emigration	imports	sovereignty
cease–fire	espionage	international	terrorism
consul	exports	nationalism	treaty
diplomacy	euro	neutrality	unification
disarmament	ideology	OPEC	
embargo	immigrant	regime	

Use the lines below to add other terms you find as you read international news stories.

Name _____

Use New Words in Sentences

Select and browse articles of international news to do the following:

   Choose ten words from **Commonly Used Terms from the International News**, or other words you find in the articles.

   Write the definitions using context clues and a dictionary for reference.

   Write your own sentence using each of the words.

Sample: *embargo: a government order prohibiting shipment of goods to another country*

The United States enforced a trade embargo against China.

....

....

....

....

....

....

....

....

....

....

....

....

....

....

Name _____

Write Meanings for New Words

Select and browse articles of international news to do the following for each of the words below:
• Locate the word, or a form of the word, in an article and copy the sentence in which it appears. For example, find *neutrality* or *neutral, immigrant* or *immigration.*
• Write the definition for each word using context clues and a dictionary for reference.
• If you are unable to locate any of the words listed, substitute a word that you find in one or more articles.

1. sovereignty

2. neutrality

3. cease-fire

4. immigrant

5. disarmament

6. diplomacy

7. espionage

8. balance of power

9. OPEC

Name _____

Read an Article about a World Event

Select and read an article of international news. Then answer the questions below.

1. Write the headline of the article on the line below.

....

2. Label the parts of speech in the headline by writing the following abbreviations above the appropriate word in the headline: **N** for nouns; **V** for verbs; **Adj** for adjectives; **Adv** for adverbs.

3. Is the headline of your article a sentence or a fragment? If it is a fragment, rewrite it to make it a complete sentence.

....

....

4. In what city does the story take place?

....

5. On which continent is the town or city where the event occurred located?

....

6. What is the main idea of the article?

....

....

7. On the lines provided, write a summary of the article. Be sure to use complete sentences.

....

....

8. Did you find any unfamiliar vocabulary words in the editorial? Write them on the lines below. Can you guess the meanings from context? Write the definition for each on the lines below. Use a dictionary if necessary.

....

....

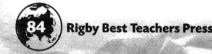

Name _____

Write a Letter to the Editor

Select and read an international news article.

Write a letter to the editor based on the article. Remember to sign your name at the bottom. Give your letter a title.

Attach the article to this sheet.

Title ....

....

....

....

....

....

....

....

....

....

....

....

....

....

....

....

....

....

....

(Your name)

....

Name _____

Around the World News

Skim international news articles for the names of foreign cities and countries. Write these names on the numbered lines below, then write the numbers in the correct locations on the map below. Use a world map or world atlas for reference.

1. Buenos Aires, Argentina   2. Belfast, Northern Ireland   3. _____

4. _____   5. _____   6. _____

7. _____   8. _____   9. _____

10. _____   11. _____   12. _____

13. _____   14. _____   15. _____

16. _____   17. _____   18. _____

19. _____   20. _____   21. _____

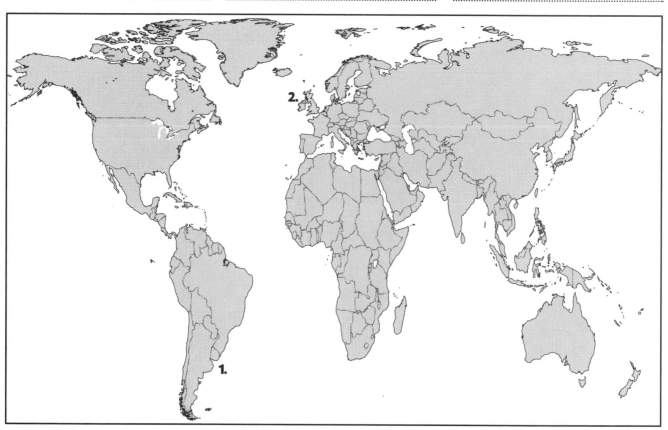

Advertising

ADVERTISING "PAYS THE BILLS" FOR NEWSPAPERS

Revenue from the sale of advertisements enables newspapers to pay the bills associated with bringing us the news. With over half of a newspaper's space filled by ads, we cannot ignore the importance of advertising to the life of a newspaper.

The reproducible reading selection **About**
Advertising is designed to be used by teachers and students alike. It provides a brief background and basic information for understanding ads in newspapers.

There are many ways in which the advertising sections of the newspaper can be used to enhance reading skills. The activities that follow
provide opportunities to do so. They include **Examining a Display Ad, Create Your Own Display Ad, Deciphering Classified Ads, Write 3 Classified Ads, Write a Letter of Application, Compare Classified and Display Ads in a Venn Diagram**, and **Compare an Antique and a Modern Ad.**

SIMULATED "ROMANCE DESIGN"

DIAMOND RINGS

$1.00 EACH OR BOTH FOR $1.79

Yellow GOLD PLATE

Matched Bridal Pair

SEND NO MONEY

South With the Sun to SAN ANTONIO

ABOUT ADVERTISING

"It pays to advertise," is a common expression that is especially true for the newspaper business. In fact, advertisements—not subscriptions—pay most of the cost of producing the newspaper. This is why many newspapers devote about 60% of their space to advertisements. Advertising pays the bills for newspapers like it does for local television programs and magazines.

Newspaper advertisements have been around for almost 500 years. The first—an ad for medicine—was printed in a German newspaper in 1525. In America, the first newspaper ads appeared in John Campbell's *Boston News-Letter* in 1704. This was the newspaper that was allowed to stay in business after it promised not to print anything objectionable to the British Crown and the Massachusetts Colonial government.

CONFUSING ADVERTISING ABBREVIATIONS DECIPHERED

The list of Common Classified Ad Abbreviations provides a reference to help decipher classifieds ads that would otherwise appear to be a jumble of typographical errors. "Sm dplx nr bch. W/D, CH/A, util incl. Sec dep req'd," for example, could be quite confusing for someone unfamiliar with terminology and abbreviations typically found in classified ads. After a brief introduction to the abbreviations on page 89, students should be able to translate that jumble into, "small duplex near the beach, with a washer and dryer, central heating and air conditioning, utilities included, security deposit required."

Name _____

Classified Ad Categories

Newspaper ads fall into two categories: classified and display. Classified ads are also called "want ads." They are placed by individuals or businesses and appear in the classified ad section of a newspaper under various subsections. These ads generally fall into one of the following categories:

Employment listings include ads about available jobs and about people seeking jobs. This section is usually broken down into several categories or headings. It may include a general listing of a variety of jobs ranging from pizza delivery to security officer. Other categories might include Office/Professional, Medical, Hotel/Motel, Restaurant, Trades/Professional, and Sales. Type of company, location, salary, and experience and qualifications may also be included in the listing.

Real Estate listings contain ads for houses and properties for sale and for rent. Ads are broken down by houses, apartments (furnished, unfurnished, efficiency, duplex, and so on), condominiums, mobile homes, and rooms to rent.

Merchandise or For Sale ads list items that individuals or businesses are offering for sale. Items can include anything from furniture and appliances to musical instruments and tools.

Other categories of ads that often appear in the classified section include Legal Notices, Personal Ads, Lost and Found, Schools/ Instruction, Wanted to Buy, Business Opportunities, Business Services, and Garage or Yard Sales.

Name _____

Display Ads and their Techniques

Display ads are large advertisements promoting a product, service, or entertainment and they usually include graphics. They come in various sizes and shapes ranging from a full page to a portion of a column. Unlike classified ads that appear in a special section of the newspaper, display ads can appear throughout the various sections, on pages that include news stories, for example. Other display ads are colorful inserts that are placed

between a newspaper's regular pages. Display ads might be for anything, but the majority focus on such products as clothing, foods, automobiles, and furniture.

The purpose of advertising is to sell the service or product advertised. Therefore, ads must call the consumers attention to the product or service and persuade them to buy it. To do this, companies use various persuasive techniques to influence the consumer. This is especially true of display ads. They include:

Testimonial. The testimonial technique involves using a well-known personality to sell a product. For example, athletes and actors frequently endorse products from personal items to cars. If the consumer respects the person who endorses the product, the consumer is likely to respect the product.

Bandwagon. The bandwagon technique convinces consumers that everyone is doing a certain thing, such as buying furniture from Slick Sam's or purchasing all their meats at Sam and Ella's Meat Market. This technique assumes that consumers want to be "just like" everyone else.

Bargain Appeal. Price reduction is used to encourage consumers to buy products and services. "Take ½ off the already low sale price." Take advantage of our "Clearance Sale". Many of us are influenced by these types of ads.

Numerical Claims. Statistics are often used to impress consumers. "Our store has been in business for over 100 years" is an ad designed to make a particular store appear more reliable than others. "More people watch Channel 5 News than all other news programs combined."

Name _____

Common Classified Ad Abbreviations

Below is a list of abbreviations that often appear in the classified ads section of a newspaper.

Familiarize yourself with these, then reference this list as you read the classified ads.

Add other abbreviations that you find on the lines provided.

1. appl—appliances
2. apt—apartment
3. BA—bathroom
4. blk—block
5. BR—bedroom
6. CH/A—central heat and air
7. condo—condominium
8. DR—dining room
9. DW—dishwasher
10. effic—efficiency apartment
11. EOE—Equal Opportunity Employer
12. exp—experience
13. flex—flexible
14. F/P—fireplace
15. F/T—full time
16. furn—furnished
17. gar—garage
18. hr—hour
19. incl—included

20. k—thousand
21. kit—kitchen
22. lg or lge—large
23. lic—license
24. LR—living room
25. MH—mobile home
26. mo—month
27. nr—near
28. P/T—part time
29. ref—references
30. req'd—required
31. sec dep— security deposit
32. scr prch—screened porch
33. sm—small
34. util—utilities
35. unfurn—unfurnished
36. w/w cpt—wall-to-wall carpets
37. W/D—washer and dryer
38. wk—week

39. W or W/—with or without
40. yr—year
41. _____
42. _____
43. _____
44. _____
45. _____
46. _____
47. _____
48. _____
49. _____
50. _____
51. _____
52. _____
53. _____
54. _____
55. _____
56. _____
57. _____

Name _____

Examining a Display Ad

Select a display ad from your local newspaper and attach it to this sheet. Read it and answer the questions about it. Remember that display ads are those large ads that often include graphics.

1. What is the name of the store or company that placed the ad?

   ....

2. Describe the store or company's logo as it appears in the ad. (Look up logo/logotype in a dictionary if you don't know the definition.)

   ....

3. What product(s) or service(s) are advertised?

   ....

   ....

4. Is the ad promoting a sale? If so, what are the dates of the sale?

   ....

   ....

5. What are the hours, phone number, and address of the store or business? Is a fax number and/or e-mail address included? If so, list this information also.

   ....

   ....

6. What prices are listed for the various products or services being advertised?

   ....

   ....

7. List any of advertising techniques used in the ad: testimonial, bandwagon, bargain appeal, and numerical claims.

   ....

   ....

Name _____

Create Your Own Display Ad

Imagine that you are the owner of Pokey Pete's Pizza Parlor or another business.

In the space below, create a display ad to appear in your local newspaper.

Remember to give your ad a logo and to include all the information that someone reading your ad would want to know.

Name _____

Deciphering Classified Ads

On the lines provided, write the complete words for each classified ad.

1. Downtown. 3 BR/2 BA
   house. W/W cpt, CH/A, F/P.
   Lge DR. $1000/mo.

2. Like new. Furn apt. 1 blk from
   beach. 2 BR/1 BA., Sec dep
   req'd.

3. Wanted exp electrician. F/T
   or P/T. Lic a must, EOE.

4. Lge MH. 2 BR/1 BA. Util incl.
   W/D, DW, $800/mo.

5. Renovated effic. Nr downtown. New appl. Sec dep and
   ref req'd.

6. P/T desk clerk. Flex hrs. Exp
   req'd. $10hr.

Name _____

Write Three Classified Ads

Imagine that you have an apartment you plan to offer for rent, a 1995 automobile (you decide the make) you wish to sell, and you are looking for a good used piano to purchase. On the lines provided, write a classified ad for each. Browse through the classified ad section of your newspaper for samples.

Remember that classified ads should be brief and to the point.

OPTIONAL ACTIVITY

Exchange your ad with a partner and rewrite your partner's ad in complete sentences.

KEYS & LOCKS
EXPERT LOCK SERVICE

Ad #1 (Apartment)

....
....
....
....
....
....

Ad #2 (Car)

....
....
....
....
....
....
....

Ad #3 (Piano)

....
....
....
....
....

Name _____

Compare Classified and Display Ads in a Venn Diagram

Fill in the Venn diagram to compare classified ads and display ads. Write facts about each in the appropriate place. List features common to both where the circles overlap.

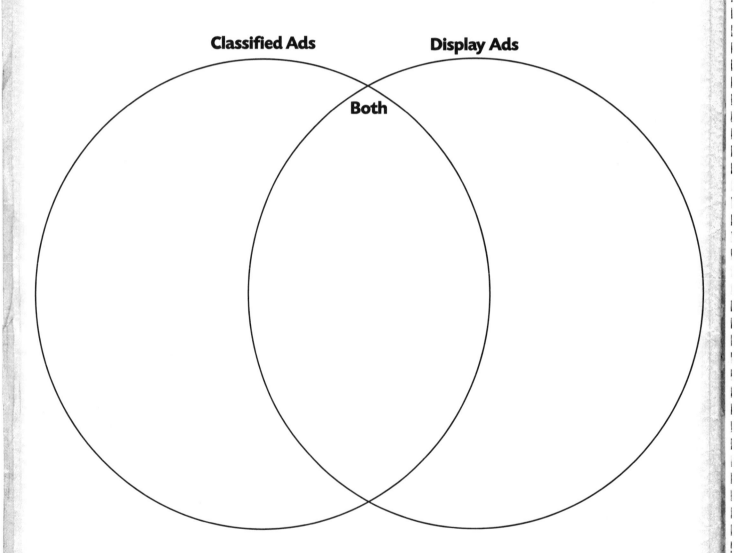

Classified Ads   **Display Ads**

Both

Name _____

Compare an Antique and a Modern Ad

Pictured below is an antique ad for footwear. Select and clip a shoe or footwear ad from a recent newspaper. Compare the ads by filling in the blanks for each shoe.

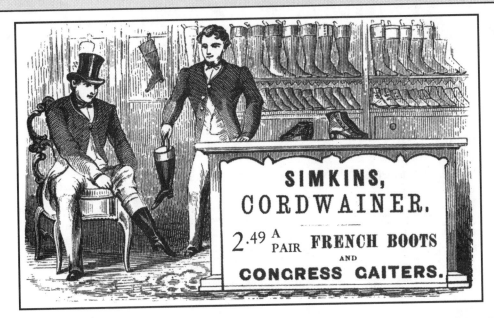

	Old Ad	**New Ad**
Company Name	....	....
Name of product	....	....
Price of product	....	....
Special features of product	....	....
Similarities between products	....	....

....

Differences between products ....

....

....

Name _____

Write a Letter of Interest for a Job Ad

Select a job ad from the Employment section of the classifieds. Write a letter expressing interest in that job.

Include your qualifications and any other information you feel will make a favorable impression on the employer.

.... (Date) ....

....

Dear _____

I am writing to express my interest in your advertised position for ....

....

....

....

....

....

....

....

....

....

....

....

....

....

The Sports Page

COLORFUL LANGUAGE BRIGHTENS SPORTSWRITING

Frequently punctuated by graphic headlines, colorful language, outrageous quotes, and well-worn cliches, sports stories and columns sometimes appeal also to readers who may not be interested in athletics, per se. Where else can you find such hyperbole as: "Bulls Gouge Celtics" and "Wildcats Skunk Crusaders?"

However, many students are, in fact, interested in sports so the sports section of the newspaper affords the teacher an excellent opportunity to develop activities that encourage reading and enhance reading skills.

Teachers will find that the headlines, the language, the cliches, and the quotes—as well as box scores, standings, and other statistics—can be used effectively in activities.

To introduce the discussion of the sports pages, share with students the following now famous quotes from sports pages by writing them on the board.

Los Angeles Lakers' Kobe Bryant skies over Phoenix Suns' Clifford Robinson (30) for two first-quarter points, Thursday, Oct. 26, 2000, in Phoenix, Ariz.

"My greatest strength is that I have no weaknesses."
—John McEnroe, former tennis champion, in the June 20, 1979, issue of the *New York Times*

"Act like you expected to get it into the end zone."
—Penn State coach Joe Paterno, commenting on some football players' excessive celebratory antics in the end zone in the October 4, 1994, issue of the *New York Times*.

"I've been here so long that when I got here, the Dead Sea wasn't even sick yet."
—Wimp Sanderson, former University of Alabama basketball coach in the May 9, 1992, issue of *Sports Illustrated*.

HYPERBOLE ENLIVENS SPORTS STORIES

HOCKEY

In addition to memorable quotes, the sport pages contain cliches, idioms, nicknames, and hyperbolic synonyms that help enliven stories and reports of games. Teams don't merely *beat* their opponents, they *annihilate*, *crush* and otherwise *trounce* them. A former Chicago Cubs' manager known for his tirades to umpires became Leo "the Lip" Durocher. Although journalism texts may have warned sports writers to avoid trite expressions and non-standard English, cliches and slang expressions still find their way into the sports sections of daily newspapers.

While the typical fan may easily understand the specialized vocabulary of a sports story, some are challenged by the unfamiliar jargon. To "drive a liner" over the centerfield fence has nothing to do with piloting a cruise ship. It is not a crime to "steal a base" and you have not lost a fight if you "go down swinging." Throwing a "bomb" is not a terrorist act and a "hat trick" is done with a stick and a puck.

The activities in this section provide students the opportunity to explore the specialized vocabulary and, style of a sports story: **Making Sense of Sports Jargon, Answer Questions About a Sports Story, Analyze the Pre-game Story** and **Write a Post-Game Story**. As in other sections of this book, activities can be done individually, in pairs, or in groups.

LET'S GO! USA

Name _____

Making Sense of Sports Jargon

Sports writers and reporters use the terms listed on these two pages when they describe football, baseball, and basketball games.

Find the meaning of each term and write it on the line beside it.

Consult friends, family members, a dictionary, or another reference book for help.

In the Add Your Own section on the next page, add other jargon you find in the paper for these sports or other sports. Write the term and the sport it references. Sample: *love: a score of zero in tennis*

Football

1. wide receiver ....

2. tight end ....

3. split end ....

4. screen pass ....

5. quarterback option ....

6. draw play ....

7. bomb ....

8. blitz ....

9. gridiron ....

10. run 'n' gun offense ....

Baseball

11. line drive ....

12. blooper ....

13. hot corner ....

14. farm team ....

Name _____

Making Sense of Sports Jargon

15. squeeze play

16. battery

17. fielder's choice

18. sacrifice

19. designated hitter

20. bean ball

Basketball Terms

21. goal-tending

22. technical foul

23. full-court-press

24. air ball

25. brick

26. run some clock (also applies to football)

27. zone defense

28. assist

29. one-and-one (referring to foul shots)

30. shot clock

31. screen

32. back court

Add Your Own

_____

_____

_____

_____

Name _____

Analyze a Pre-Game Story

POLAR BEARS PREPARE FOR CHAMPIONSHIP FACE-OFF

by Fred Fumble

"Less talk, more play," warned Coach Art Arctic after his Polar Bears froze out Tundra Tech in last week's conference semi-final. "Next stop, Sleetville."

According to Arctic, the Polar Bears' huge win over TT is no guarantee of victory in Saturday's championship game with Sleetville. "Sleetville is still stinging from that whipping we gave them last year," said Arctic "They'll be looking to settle the score on their home turf next week."

Most observers feel that Coach Arctic's fears are ungrounded. In recent weeks, his Polar Bears throttled Snow City 42-7, trounced Frigid Falls 49-3, and annihilated Beaver Crossing 63-0. Does Sleetville belong on the same field with such a juggernaut?

This writer thinks so. Sleetville is led by the most prolific passer in conference history, Tommy "Rifle" Timmons. All the "Rifle" did this season was set new conference records in passes attempted and passes completed. In 10 games, he has completed some 66% of his passes, hitting on 205 out of 301 attempts. Of his 205 completions, 39 have gone for touchdowns.

Timmons favorite target has been wide receiver Oscar "Blue Streak" Otis. Otis has recorded over 50 receptions, 21 of which have been for touchdowns. In the game against out-manned Frigid Falls, Otis caught 5 touchdown passes.

On defense, Sleetville is led by linebacker Billy "Bull" Bevins. Bevins leads the conference in both tackles and sacks. At 6'6" and 265 pounds, the Bull has

probably made more than one receiver wish he had stuck with the band.

The Polar Bears will counter Sleetville's potent attack with the power running of Ted "Truck" Timmons, talented brother of Sleetville's QB. When asked which team his parents would be cheering for on Saturday, Ted replied, "The team with the best Timmons."

Provided the present blizzard eases and the dog teams can get through, some 30,000 fans are expected to show up at Sleetville's Iceberg Field Saturday for this conference donnybrook.

How does your scribe here see it? A close one, to be sure, but the Polar Bears should prevail by a touchdown.

The call: Frostburg 27, Sleetville 20

Name _____

Analyze a Pre-Game Story

On the previous page is a pre-game story about an imaginary upcoming game.
Read it carefully and answer the **Analyze a Pre-game Story** questions.

1. What sport is the story about? Although the sport is not mentioned by name, what clues are given?

....

2. Which two teams are playing for the conference championship?

....

....

3. What are the meanings of the words "juggernaut," and "donnybrook?" Try to discover the meaning from the context. Then confirm the meanings using the dictionary.

....

....

....

4. What do you think their nicknames say about each of the following players?

"Rifle" Timmons

....

"Blue Streak" Otis

....

"Bull" Bevins

....

"Truck" Timmons

5. Is the writer's report unbiased, or does it favor one team? Explain your answer.

....

....

....

....

Name _____

Answer Questions About a Sports Story

Select and read a sports story about a recent game. It can be any team sport at the professional or school level.

Answer the following questions.

1. What is the headline on the story?

   ....

   ....

   ....

2. Is the headline a complete sentence or a fragment? If it is a fragment, rewrite it to make it a complete sentence.

   ....

   ....

   ....

3. Who is the writer?

   ....

4. Is the report about a local, state, or national contest?

   ....

5. What are the names of the teams that were involved?

   ....

6. Who were the outstanding players for both teams? What, if any, are the players' nicknames?

   ....

   ....

7. Which team won the game, and what was the final score?

   ....

8. What was the turning point of the game?

   ....

   ....

9. What colorful language and special jargon were used in the story?

   ....

   ....

10. What synonyms are used for defeat, win, or lose?

   ....

   ....

11. In your opinion, did the writer's report accurately describe the game? Was it unbiased, or did it favor one team over the other? Explain.

   ....

   ....

   ....

Name _____

Write a Post-Game Story

Imagine you are a sports writer assigned to write a post-game story on a game or sporting event. It can be one you played in, one that was played at your school, or an imaginary one.

Write a story about the game or event. You may base it on an interview with one of the players or coaches, or other information related to the game or event.

Information for your story can come from a newspaper write-up of a recent sporting event.

Use the back of this page if necessary.

Headline:

....

....

by ....

....

....

....

....

....

....

....

....

....

....

....

....

....

....

....

....

....

....

....

....

TRAVEL by BUS

Television and Entertainment

ENTERTAINMENT REPORTING OFFERS LIGHTER FARE

Where and when are the latest movies playing? What concerts are in the area? Is a certain play worth seeing? What's on television tonight? What's a good restaurant for taking guests?

While some people check the sports pages of their newspaper daily to see how their favorite teams are faring, others head for the television and entertainment section to answer the above questions and find other useful—but not necessarily essential—information. Here they find such information as current television schedules and movie listings, the latest music and video releases, art and museum exhibits, restaurant listings, features stories by entertainment writers, reviews by entertainment critics, the daily horoscope, and often the latest scoop about entertainment celebrities. Some newspapers may include book news and reviews in entertainment sections while others include these in a special book section.

Reviews, like columns and editorials, contain the opinions of the writers. They also include facts about the movie, the music, or other item being reviewed—especially facts that support the reviewers opinion. Like sports stories and columns, reviews are frequently full of colorful language. Many reviewers use a "4-star" rating system, with four stars ★★★★ being the best possible and no stars being the worst.

While daily news reports usually focus on serious issues from global to local, the entertainment section often provides more light-hearted fare. Often the information on celebrities and upcoming entertainment programs, events, and places is entertainment in and of itself. For example, while stories of the latest celebrity exploits may not be important news, they often attract attention and are popular with many readers. Consider the following imaginary news flash from Hollywood.

ROMEO APARTMENT HUNTING

LOS ANGELES—With the ink barely dry on the prenuptial agreement, Sallie Sue Shapely, sizzling star of stage and screen, and her husband of five hours, Ricardo Romeo, have separated. Romeo, who claimed he had given in to many of Shapely's demands and overlooked her idiosyncrasies, drew the line when it came to her 25 Irish wolfhounds. "Either those dogs go or I go!" Romeo declared, waving his fists into the air for emphasis. Shapely later told reporters that she wished Romeo well in his search for new living quarters.

HOROSCOPE PROVIDES AMUSEMENT, GUIDANCE

Another popular item included in many newspaper entertainment sections is the daily horoscope. Many ancient rulers consulted astrologers before making important decisions. Nowadays most people read horoscopes as a form of amusement; however, some have taken them seriously in more modern times. Hitler's Propaganda Minister Joseph Goebbels truly thought that the stars foretold events to come. When President Franklin Roosevelt died in April, 1945, Goebbels triumphantly announced that it fulfilled a prophecy and boded well for Germany. More recently, the wife of an American president was known to consult with an astrologer.

From those who are looking for something to do in their leisure time to those who are just looking for a good laugh, readers will find a variety of interesting items in the television and entertainment section of the daily newspaper.

The television and entertainment section provides a variety of lively reading selections that lend themselves to number of enjoyable activities. Provided on the following pages are **Comment on a Celebrity Story, Analyze a Movie Review, Critique a Movie Review, Pre-Review Checklist, Write a Review**, and **Fill in a Venn Diagram**. These may be done individually, in pairs, or in groups and may be posted or shared orally with the class.

OPTIONAL ACTIVITIES

• Contact your local paper for information on making student submissions to the entertainment section. Have students write movie, book, music, theater, restaurant or other entertainment reviews for a local newspaper. Always secure the proper student and parental permission before submitting student work for publication.

• Have students read about and share information about the constellations of the zodiac, as well as the symbols of the Chinese zodiac.

• Have students write their own horoscopes based on existing or invented signs of the zodiac.

Name _____

Comment on a Celebrity Story

Select and read a story about a celebrity from the entertainment section of a newspaper.

Answer the questions below.

Attach the story to this sheet.

1. What is the headline on the story?

....

2. Who wrote the story?

....

3. What is the name of the celebrity featured in the story?

....

4. What is the occupation of the celebrity? (movie actor, stage actor, musician, songwriter, or other)

....

5. What is the main idea of the story?

....

....

6. What facts about the celebrity appear in the story?

....

....

7. What opinions about the celebrity appear in the story?

....

....

8. Did you enjoy the story? Why or why not?

....

....

Name _____

Analyze a Movie Review

BAN THE BROCCOLI

reviewed by Freddy Flick
What a loser! *Attack of the Alien Broccoli* features a bunch of silly middle-school kids being terrorized by an even sillier bunch of giant broccoli clusters. The broccoli clusters have arrived from some distant planet to take revenge on the kids for all the nasty things they have said about broccoli in the past. Kids who are slow afoot are trampled and squashed by the angry giant clusters; those who survive are traumatized for life. In the end, the nasty green invaders agree to go away if every kid on earth promises to eat broccoli at least once a week.

I have to admit that the Sears Tower-sized leader of the broccoli clusters was an incredible graphic, but give me a break! Alien broccoli invaders, indeed! Kids, avoid this no-brainer. Save your money for something better, like next week's coming attraction at the Bijou Theater: *Revenge of the Underpaid Babysitters*.

Rating: ★

Read the imaginary review above, then answer the questions about it.

1. What is the title of the movie reviewed?
....

2. What is the name of the reviewer?
....

3. Briefly tell what the movie is about.
....
....

4. Did the reviewer like the movie? What words or phrases does he use to express his opinion?
....
....

5. After reading this review, would you go to see this movie? Why or why not?
....
....

Name _____

Critique a Movie Review

Select and read from the entertainment section of a newspaper a review of one of the following:

• a movie, video, play, or other performance you have seen

• a CD you have heard

• a book you have read

• a restaurant where you have eaten

• an art or museum exhibit you have visited

Compare your opinion to the opinion of the reviewer by answering the following questions.

Attach the newspaper review to this sheet.

1. What is being reviewed in the article?

....

2. Who wrote the review?

....

3. What is the reviewer's opinion? What specifically did the reviewer like or dislike?

....

....

4. What words or phrases are used to express the reviewer's opinion?

....

....

5. Do you agree with the reviewer's opinion? Explain.

....

....

6. Rewrite this review to express your opinion and rating of this item.

....

....

....

....

....

....

Name _____

Pre-Review Checklist

Imagine that you are the entertainment reporter for a newspaper.

Fill in the checklist below to help you write a review of a movie, video, music CD, play, book, exhibit, or other type of performance.

Title:

Check one: movie   video   music CD

            play   book   exhibit

other, please specify

Artist or performer (if applicable)

Specific things I liked about it and why

Specific things I did not like about it and why

Summary of my opinion in 1-2 sentences

Statement of my recommendation

My rating (using 4-star or other system)

Rigby Best Teachers Press

Name _____

Write a Review

Using the information from your **Pre-Review Checklist**, write a review.

Optional: With your parent's permission and your teacher's help, submit the review to your local newspaper.

Headline: ....

....

....

....

....

....

....

....

....

....

....

....

....

....

....

....

....

....

(your name)

....

Name _____

Fill in a Venn Diagram

Fill in the Venn diagram to compare the entertainment pages of small town and large city newspapers. Write facts about each in the appropriate place. List features common to both where the circles overlap.

Small Town Newspapers

Large City Newspapers

Both

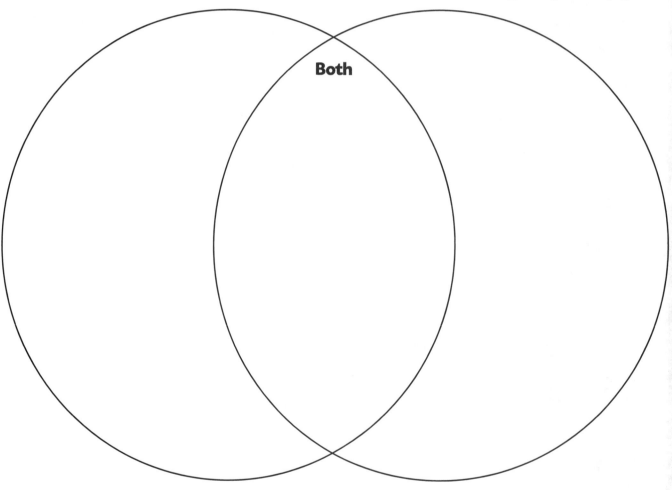

CHAPTER TEN

The Comics

COMICS PAGE FAVORITE FOR READERS OF ALL AGES

Who hasn't laughed at one of Snoopy's air assaults on the infamous Red Baron or grinned when Garfield once again tricked the gullible Odie? To be sure, life would go on without "Dilbert," "Peanuts," "The Wizard of Id," and your favorite comic, but would it be as much fun?

Actually, the therapeutic value of laughter began to get serious attention in medical research studies after *Saturday Review* editor Norman Cousins attributed his recovery from a type of arthritis to watching his favorite humorous videos. While the health benefits of the comics section may be difficult to measure, a favorite comic affords for many readers a chuckle or two that helps relieve some of the daily tensions.

Although it may not hold the cure for all ills, the comics section of the newspaper is a favorite with readers of all ages. This popularity makes it a logical prescription for motivating students to read.

Have you ever wondered how the comic strips got started? Do you think they go back many years, or would you guess—considering how long newspapers have been around—that they are relatively new? Reproduce **A Brief History of the Comics** and use it as a reading selection to begin your adventure with the comics section of the newspaper.

The first activity is **Understanding A Brief History of the Comics.** The activities that follow require exploration of the comics section of the newspaper—something most students will not need much encouragement to do. Included are: **Explore a Comic Strip, Describe a Comic Strip Character, Draw a Comic Strip Character, Categorize Comic Strips, Identify Parts of Speech in Comics**, and **Create a Cartoon or Comic Strip**. These activities can be done individually, in pairs, or in groups. Students will especially enjoy sharing them with the class.

Sjoerdsma comic. Reprinted by permission.

A BRIEF HISTORY OF THE COMICS

Cartoons and caricatures have been around for several hundred years, but the first newspaper comic strip did not appear until almost the end of the 19th century. On February 17, 1895, "Hogan's Alley" appeared in Joseph Pulitzer's *New York World*. It was drawn by Richard F. Outcault, was set in the slums of New York City, and featured the Yellow Kid, a bald, big-eared, goofy youngster who wore a yellow nightshirt and did funny things. Because the word *comic* is derived from a Greek word meaning "something that produces laughter," the escapades of the Yellow Kid and similar characters that followed led to the comic page being called the "funny page" by many people.

In the beginning, comics strips were just meant to be funny. Such classics as the "Katzenjammer Kids" (1897) and "Mutt and Jeff" (1909) were all created to tickle the funny bone. So were "Bringing Up Father"

(1913) and "The Gumps" (1917). By the end of the 1920s, however, different kinds of comic strips began to appear. These were the action-packed comics that began with "Dick Tracy" in 1931 and included such well-known strips as "Superman," "Flash Gordon," "Terry and the Pirates," and "Steve Canyon." Instead of relating a different story everyday, the action-packed comics continued with the same story for days and even weeks. When a story was brought to a conclusion, a new story began.

The goal of many of today's comic strips—like the goal of the earliest ones—is to make people laugh. However, other

modern comic strips focus on making a statement about serious issues.

Many modern comic strips portray everyday people and their daily lives. They are created by cartoonists who draw from their own experiences. These comic strips are often funny, but also portray tender, sad, or other kinds of experiences that are not humorous. Charles Schultz's beloved "Peanuts"—which debuted on October 2, 1950—is a well-known example of this type of comic strip. Schultz readily admitted that Good Ol' Charlie Brown was nothing more than a personification of himself as a young boy.

Bringing Up Father, by George McManus, 1918.

Name _____

Understanding "A Brief History of the Comics"

Read "A Brief History of the Comics," and then answer the questions on this page.

Use the "Brief History" for reference.

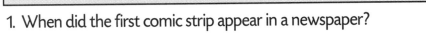

1. When did the first comic strip appear in a newspaper?

....

2. What was the name of the comic strip and who was the main character in it?

....

3. Which well-known comic strip debuted on October 2, 1950?

....

4. What was the name of the first action-packed comic strip?

....

5. Why is the comics section of the newspaper called the "funny pages"?

....

6. Are all comic strips funny? Explain.

....

....

7. Why do you think comic strips are so popular?

....

....

8. Are any of the comic strips mentioned in the brief history still around today in one form or another? Name any of them you can find.

....

....

Name _____

Explore a Comic Strip

Select and read a comic strip from the newspaper, and then answer the questions below.

   Attach the comic strip to this sheet.

1. Who is the main character?

   ....

2. Is the main character a human being, an animal, or other creature?

   ....

3. Describe how the main character looks.

   ....

4. Describe the personality of the main character

   ....

5. What is the main character's role in the comic strip?

   ....

6. Name one or more important characters besides the main character.

   ....

7. Who is your favorite character? Why?

   ....

   ....

   ....

8. What kind of comic strip is it? (for example: funny, a story, one with a message, an action series) Explain.

   ....

   ....

   ....

9. Would it appeal to people of a particular age or to people of all ages? Explain.

   ....

   ....

   ....

©2001 Rigby

Name _____

Describe a Comic Strip Character

Select and view one or more newspaper comic strips.

Choose three characters from the strip or strips and describe each of them at right. Include information about physical appearance, personality, and role in the comic strip. Use these descriptions to help you draw the characters in the boxes on the next page.

Character #1: Name ....

Description ....

....

....

....

....

....

Character #2: Name ....

Description ....

....

....

....

....

....

Character #3: Name ....

Description ....

....

....

....

....

RRR

Name _____

Draw a Comic Strip Character

In three of the boxes below, draw each of the three characters you described. You may color the pictures if you choose. In the fourth box draw a character you create.

Rigby Best Teachers Press

Name _____

Categorize Comic Strips

You have learned that comic strips come in all "shapes and sizes." Some tell a different story every day, while others continue for days or weeks. Some focus on important issues; others poke fun at the trials and problems of everyday life. Many are simply meant to be funny and have no particular message in mind.

Look at a newspaper's comic pages for several days to compare the comic strips.

Then answer the questions on this page.

1. Write the names of two comic strips that have a continuing story and the names of the cartoonists who created them.

....

....

2. Name a comic strip in which an animal is the main character and the name of the cartoonist who created it.

....

....

3. Name any two comic strips that poke fun at everyday life and the names of the cartoonists who created them. Explain what everyday life situations are featured in each one.

....

....

....

....

....

4. Write the name of a comic that is always drawn in just one panel and the name of the creator.

....

....

5. Which comic do you think is the best? Why?

....

....

....

Name _____

Identify Parts of Speech in Comics

Select four comics from the daily newspaper.
   List each of the words in the comics on the lines below the appropriate parts of speech.
   Attach the four comics to this sheet.

Nouns	**Verbs**	**Pronouns**	**Adjectives**

Adverbs	**Prepositions**	**Conjunctions**	**Interjections**

 Rigby Best Teachers Press

Name _____

Create a Cartoon or Comic Strip

Have you ever wanted to draw a cartoon or comic strip? Are you good at doodling and drawing stick figures? Do you have a funny message you would like to relate through simple pictures or something you would like to poke fun at in a good-natured way? Here's your chance. Create your own cartoon or a segment of a comic strip. Look at the comic page of your local newspaper for ideas. Remember that cartoons and comic strips come in all varieties.

CHAPTER ELEVEN

Other Pages

BUSINESS, GARDENING, HEALTH COVERED BY MOST PAPERS

The format, arrangement, and inclusion of special sections vary from newspaper to newspaper. Most papers include editorials, sports, comics, entertainment, advertisements, and news on the local, state, national, and international levels. However, newspapers may differ considerably on a variety of other sections. Many will have, for example, a separate business section, while others will include information about the stock market, business trends, and mergers within another part of the newspaper. Special sections featuring gardening, food, health and fitness, homes, and autos appear in some newspapers, while others include articles and information about these within other sections. For these reasons, a number of topics covered in a variety of areas are combined in this final chapter called "Other Pages."

Activities for three of these sections follow: gardening, food, and business/financial. You are encouraged to explore other appropriate sections with your students. Use the activities in this chapter and in previous chapters as models for developing activities for the other sections.

Special sections of the *Detroit Free Press*.

Rigby Best Teachers Press

GREEN THUMBS DEVELOPED

The gardening section appeals to readers who want to develop or improve their "green thumbs." This part of the newspaper may be both fascinating and amusing. This is not surprising when one considers some of the letters sent to and responses composed by the local horticulturist. It is not unusual to see letters like the following:

The Popular but Particular Potato and **Skim a Gardening Article** provide the opportunity for students to practice skimming for information. Other activities in this section include: **Perusing the Food Section, Commonly Used Terms from the Business News,** and **Use New Sentences.**

Ask the Plant Doctor

Dear Plant Doctor,
My prized Formosa azalea, which I raised from infancy and which had reached a height of over 10 feet, has lost all of its leaves. It looks like a bunch of sticks just poking out of the ground. I have watered and fertilized but I see no positive results. What can I do to restore my once healthy plant to its natural beauty?

Mrs. H.

Dear Mrs. H.
I'm sad to inform you that your prized Formosa azalea has departed this world. My advice is to go to your favorite nursery and adopt a new one. Let me know if I can be of further assistance.

The Plant Doctor

OPTIONAL ACTIVITIES:
• Select a brief announcement of an upcoming flower or plant show to read aloud to students. Before you read it to them, tell them they are to listen for and to record the days, hours, and location of the show and any other information that tells what visitors can expect. Have them write a paragraph about the show using the notes they took.

• Have students read a column or article that explains how to plant and/or care for a particular shrub, tree, vegetable, or flower, then list the steps in sequential order.

Name _____

The Popular but Particular Potato

by Hannah Horticulturist

America's favorite vegetable, the potato, is grown in all 50 states and is prepared in many ways. From the ever-popular French fry to the most basic boiled variety, potatoes in one form or another can be found on most dinner tables throughout the country.

The potato is popular on the menu; however it is not a popular crop in the home garden. This may be because it requires more care than many other vegetables usually grown in backyard gardens. For those who are willing to spend a little extra time, the rewards of growing potatoes are worth the effort. Here is some basic information you should consider before you add them to your garden.

Potatoes need to be planted in an area of the garden that gets plenty of sun. The soil should be sandy, well drained, and rich in organic matter. Seed potatoes labeled "certified" are the best for planting—not cooking potatoes from a grocery store. This will help insure that they are disease free and are of a variety that grows well in your area.

To prepare seed potatoes for planting, first cut off the ends, then cut the remaining part into 4 parts. Place the parts in a sunny place for 4–5 days. Dig furrows 6–8 inches wide, 3–4 inches deep, and 3 feet apart. Put fertilizer in each furrow; then plant the seed potatoes 12–15 inches apart. Cover them with 3 inches of soil.

Planting should be done in the spring when there is no danger of frost. When the plants have grown to 10 inches tall, make a soil mound 3–4 inches tall around each plant.

Protecting the plants from pests and diseases and keeping the garden weed-free are other challenges for potato growers. There are both natural and chemical ways to care for your garden.

If you have decided that potato growing is for you, please send a self-addressed, stamped envelope to P.O. Box 555, Anytown, USA, for a free brochure on growing and harvesting potatoes.

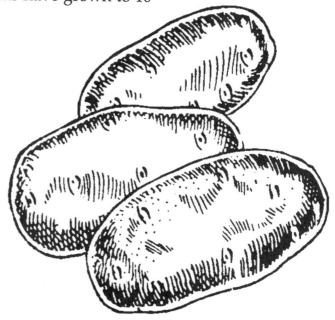

Name _____

Skim a Gardening Article

Read the questions below before reading **The Popular but Particular Potato** article.

Skim the article to find the answers to the questions. Answer from memory as many of the questions as you can.

Refer back to the article if you need help in answering the questions.

1. What is the headline?

....

....

2. Who is the author?

....

....

3. What kind of plant was discussed in the article?

....

....

4. When should the plant be planted?

....

....

5. On the lines below, list other information about the plant found in the article.

....

....

....

....

- Now select an article about gardening from the newspaper.
- Before reading the article, read the questions below.
- Skim the article to find the answers to the questions.
- Answer from memory as many of the questions as you can.
- Refer back to the article if you need help in answering the questions.

6. What is the headline?

....

7. Who is the author?

....

8. What kind of plant was discussed in the article?

....

9. When should the plant be planted?

....

10. On the lines below, list other information about the plant found in the article.

....

....

....

....

FOOD SECTIONS OFFER "SOMETHING FOR EVERYONE"

In the food section, budget gourmets and connoisseurs alike can find everything from the lowest prices offered at the local supermarkets to recipes for preparing the most scrumptious of meals. Everyone eats; there is likely something for everyone on the food pages. Recipes, for example, contain measurements. What is the difference between a teaspoon and a tablespoon? How much is $\frac{1}{2}$ cup of something, and can any cup be used in measuring? Just how much equals a serving, or how much is a "pinch" of salt? What country is that recipe from?

A variety of recipes from main courses to desserts, from low fat to high cholesterol, can be found in newspapers. Like sports stories, food articles have a colorful vocabulary all their own.

Reading selections from this section often lend themselves well to interdisciplinary use.

OPTIONAL ACTIVITIES:

• Have students prepare a recipe at home with the help of a parent or other adult, then write a review of the recipe and the food.

• Have students find a "healthy" recipe and then write an advertisement for the food that makes it sound appealing.

• Have students plan a meal using recipes from the food section.

• Have students choose a recipe, find the prices for each of the ingredients in a grocery store, and estimate the cost of preparing the dish.

Name _____

Perusing the Food Section

Using the food section of the newspaper, answer the following questions.

1. How many types of recipes can you find in this section? Circle all that apply.

appetizer   main course

vegetable   salad

dessert   beverage

other

2. List the adjectives used to describe the foods in the articles and recipes.

....

....

....

....

3. List the verbs used to describe the procedures in the recipes.

....

....

....

....

4. Do any of the recipes come from foreign countries? If so, list the name of the food and the country.

....

5. Choose a recipe and use the staircase below to list the steps to prepare it. If there are more than five steps, combine two or more steps on some of the stairs.

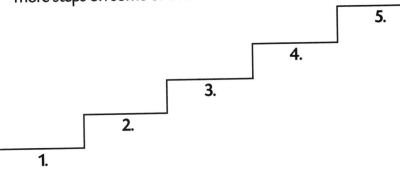

6. Choose a recipe you would like to prepare and pretend your cooking supplies are low. You will only have enough ingredients to make half of the recipe. List all of the ingredients and the amounts on the lines below. Then divide the amounts in half and write these amounts next to the ingredients. For example, $1/2$ cup of flour becomes $1/4$ cup.

....

....

....

....

7. What is your favorite recipe in this section? Why?

....

....

....

BUSINESS PAGES OFFER WIDE RANGE OF COVERAGE

A final part of the newspaper worthy of attention is the business section. The space given to this section may vary from one to several pages in small newspapers to almost 30 pages in a big-city newspaper. While smaller newspapers might focus mainly on the stock market, with a few columns and briefs about trends and sales, larger newspapers usually run the gamut of business news from "A" to "Z." The *New York Times*, for example, in addition to keeping the reader informed about the ups and downs of the stock market, might devote considerable space to such matters as online investments, job announcements, company news, and even fitness clubs for CEOs. Its pages also include advertisements ranging from copy machines to conducting businesses via the Internet.

How much class time you choose to devote to the business page will depend, of course, on the interest and abilities of your students, as well as your own familiarity with the subject. You may at least want to assign a few articles to be read for comprehension and discussion. Before doing so, however, it will be helpful to go over some commonly used terms.

> **OPTIONAL ACTIVITIES:**
> Read an article or column about the merger or the proposed merger of two businesses or companies. Then discuss the following:
> • What are the names of the companies?
> • What is the nature of the companies' businesses?
> • Why is the merger proposed?
> • How will the merger affect employment for both companies?
> • What impact will the merger have on the economy?
>
> Have students select a company whose product they buy and follow the progress of its stock on either the Nasdaq or the New York Stock Exchange for one week or more. Have them graph or write a summary of their observations.

Name _____

Commonly Used Terms from the Business News

Below are some of the terms that can be found in the business news and basic definitions for each.

Find definitions for the four terms listed. Use the lines below to add others found in your reading.

balanced budget: a budget in which receipts equal expenditures

bear market: a market characterized by falling stock prices

bull market: a market characterized by rising stock prices

common stock: ordinary stock in a company that has no guaranteed rate of dividend

blue chip stock: generally stable stock from a well established company characterized by public confidence in its worth

dividend: payment made by a corporation or business to its stockholders

preferred stock: stock on which dividends are paid at a predetermined rate

bond: a paper promising to pay back with interest money that has been lent

cost of living: the cost of maintaining a standard of living measured against the cost of goods and services

consumer price index (CPI): an index that measures changes in the costs of goods and services for the typical wage earner—also called cost-of-living index

Dow Jones Industrial Average: an index of the stock prices of 30 leading companies on the Nasdaq (National Association of Securities Dealers) and the New York Stock Exchange

individual retirement account (IRA): a savings account in which a limited amount of wages can be deposited tax free and held until retirement

inflation: a condition of rising prices and interest rates.

interest: a charge paid for borrowed money or money earned on deposited money

liquid assets: assets consisting of either cash or of items that can be easily converted into cash

recession: a temporary period of slower economic activity

merger ....

....

monopoly ....

....

antitrust ....

....

downsizing ....

....

....

....

....

....

....

Use New Words in Sentences

Select and browse articles from the business news. Choose six words from **Commonly Used Terms** and find them on the Business/Financial Page of the newspaper.

For each word, copy the sentence in which the word occurs and underline the word in the sentence.

Write your own sentence using each of the words.

Sample:

"The proposed <u>merger</u> of Ma Kettle's Tea Terrace and Papa's Cappuccino Cafes has been approved by the Federal Trade Commission, a move that will open the door for a nationwide chain of hot beverage franchises."

A <u>merger</u> of all the fast food restaurants could result in higher priced hamburgers.

Additional Resources

Adams, Julian, and Kenneth Stratton. *Press Time.* Englewood Cliffs, New Jersey: Prentice-Hall, Inc., 1985.

Carney, Debra. *Using the Newspaper to Teach Reading Skills.* Westminster, California: Teacher Created Materials, 1999.

Discovering America's Past: Customs, Legends, History and Lore of Our Great Nation. New York: The Reader's Digest Association, Inc., 1993.

Ferguson, Donald L. and Jim Patten. *Journalism Today.* Lincolnwood, Illinois: National Textbook Company, 1986.

Fountas, I. C. and G. S. Pinnell. *Guided Reading: Good First Teaching for All Children.* Portsmouth, New Hampshire: Heinemann, 1996.

Fredericks, Anthony. *Guided Reading in Grades 3–6: A Ready Resource for the Busy Teacher.* Barrington, IL: Rigby, 2001.

Visser, Evangelyn, and Gary M. Hanggi. *Guided Reading in a Balanced Program.* Westminster, California: Teacher Created Materials, 1999.

ONLINE EDITIONS OF MAJOR CITY NEWSPAPERS

Chicago Tribune:
http://www.chicagotribune.com

Christian Science Monitor:
http://www.csmonitor.com

Daily Telegraph of London:
http://www.telegraph.co.uk

Dallas Morning News:
http://www.dallasnews.com

Los Angeles Times:
http://www.latimes.com

New York Times:
http://www.nytimes.com

San Francisco Chronicle:
http://www.sfgate.com/chronicle

The Times of London:
http:www.thetimes.co.uk

Wall Street Journal:
http://www.intereactive.wsj.com

FOR GEOGRAPHY REFERENCES AND OTHER INFORMATION ABOUT COUNTRIES IN THE NEWS:

Yahooligans is a student-friendly site. Click on "social studies" under the "School Bell" heading: **http://www. yahooligans. com**

The Central Intelligence Agency site provides detailed and up-to-date information on nations of the world: **http://www. odci.gov/cia/publications/ factbook**

For information about the Newspaper in Education (NIE) program of the Newspaper Association of America Foundation: **http://www.naa. org/foundation/index.html**

Add the addresses of your local newspapers and other useful Internet resources on the lines below.

Answers to Activities

Chapter 1, "The Newspaper Adventure"

page 11, *Write a Letter to the Royal Governor:* Reasons will vary but may include mention of freedom of the press, geographical distance between England and America, personal freedom, injustice of the British government.

pages 16–17, *Conduct a Survey About Newspaper Readership:* Answers will vary.

page 18, *Complete a Newspaper Timeline:* 1690, publication of first American newspaper, *Public Occurrences Both Foreign and Domestick*; 1704, *Boston News-Letter* is published; 1719, *American Weekly Mercury* founded; 1721, *New England Courant* founded; 1833, *New York Sun* founded; 1841, *New York Tribune* founded; 1851, *New York Times* founded; 1880-1890, presses were bigger and faster and photographs began to appear; 1896, the Yellow Kid first appeared; 1920, more than 2,000 dailies in America; 1950s, television contributed to newspaper decline; 1990s, laptops and modems help reporters; 1997, about 1,500 dailies in America.

page 19, *Fill in a Venn Diagram:* Students' answers will vary but might include: Early Newspapers: focused on business and politics; were expensive; consisted of only a few pages; not widely read; had little local news. Both: report on political events, business happenings; separate from the government. Modern Newspapers: have many sections: editorial, sports, entertainment, and so on; contain many pages; are affordable; cover local news; have online editions; have current news.

page 23, *Explore Your News Knowledge:* Answers will vary (see discussion, pages 21-22).

page 24, *Fill in a Venn Diagram:* Answers will vary.

page 25, *Practicing with Headlines:* Answers will vary.

page 27, *Dissecting Front Page News:* Answers will vary.

page 29, *The Anywhere Tribune:* Answers will vary.

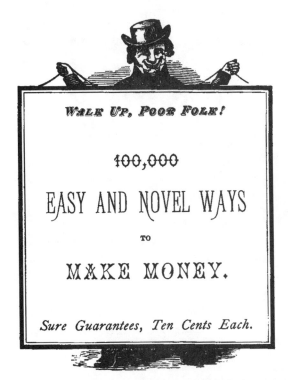

WAKE UP, POOR FOLK!

100,000

EASY AND NOVEL WAYS

TO

MAKE MONEY.

Sure Guarantees, Ten Cents Each.

Chapter 2, "The Front Page and News"

page 31–32, Identify Topic Sentences: First article: "Everyone seemed enthralled at the sight of the mother duck and her four fluffy ducklings waddling across the intersection." Second article: "Democratic candidate Yancy Yakker isn't difficult to spot." Third article: "Daredevil Dan, the plane's pilot, was lucky to be alive." Fourth article: "The storm wreaked havoc on the downtown area."

page 34, Adding a Topic Sentence: **First article:** Answers will vary but will be similar to, "Voters support Yancy Yakker for a number of reasons." **Second article:** answers will vary. They may include a description of any amusing situation that would stop traffic.

Chapter 3, "The Editorial Page"

page 39, The What and Why of the Masthead: Answers will vary.

page 40, What Is It?: 1. letter to the editor; 2. editorial; 3. letter to the editor; 4. editorial; 5. column

page 42, Read and Interpret an Editorial: 1. Some laws are not fair and should be changed. 2. A zoning ordinance against operating an animal shelter. 3. Answers will vary. 4. Answers will vary. 5. Answers will vary. 6. Answers will vary. 7. Answers will vary.

page 43, Read and Interpret an Editorial: Choose Your Own: Answers will vary.

page 47, Read and Interpret a Column:
Remembering "A Matter of Values": 1. Speedy Hinson; 2. 3 years; 3. Colossal Studios, $2.5 million; 4. *Wow Magazine*; 5. $30,000; $28,000

page 48, Read and Interpret a Column: Thinking about "A Matter of Values": 1. Public employees are paid too little for their work, especially compared to athletes and actors. 2–4. Answers will vary.

page 49, Read and Interpret a Column: Choose Your Own Column: Answers will vary.

page 52, Interpret a Letter to the Editor: Thinking About "About Old Glory": 1. Many people do not show respect for the American flag. 2. Answers will vary. 3. Answers will vary. 4. <u>Opinions</u>: What they *didn't* do was show proper respect for our flag. In the eyes of everyone else, the American flag passing by was no different from the flags carried by the twirlers of our local high school band. Any American who doesn't understand or appreciate that fact needs to re-enroll in American History 101. Otherwise, we are not worthy of all the right and freedoms associated with it. <u>Facts</u>: Thousands of American men and boys have died defending that *thing*; Even during colonial days, others fought and died to assure that that *thing* would become a reality. 5. Answers will vary.

page 53, Interpret a Letter to the Editor: Choose Your Own: Answers will vary.

page 55, Interpret a Political Cartoon: 1. The colonies had little chance of survival unless they joined together for their defense. 2. Answers will vary. 3. There was little cooperation between the colonies.

page 56, Interpret a Political Cartoon: Choose Your Own: Answers will vary.

page 57, Review of the Editorial Page: 1. An editorial represents the views of the newspaper; a column represents the views of an individual columnist. 2. No. Letters that are not signed or have no address and phone number, that are obscene or threatening, or are considered inappropriate may not be printed. 3. Answers will vary. 4. They may contain facts to support the opinion of the writer. 5. Look up the words or ask someone who knows. Otherwise you won't understand the column or editorial.

Chapter 4, "Local and State News"

page 61, Examining a Local or State News Story: Answers will vary.

page 62, Share New Vocabulary Words: Answers will vary.

page 65, Know Your Prefixes: Answers will vary. 1. self; 2. badly; ill; 3. badly; poorly; 4. one; 5. many; 6. before; 7. across, over, through; 8. again, back; 9. under, below; 10. half 11. not; 12. within; 13. in, into; 14. not; 15. too little; 16. good; 17. with; 18. among, between

page 66, Use Prefixes in Words: Answers will vary.

Chapter 5, "The National Scene"

page 69, Commonly Used Terms from the National News: Answers will vary.

page 74, Examining a National News Article: 1. Gun control is a controversial issue that will continue to be debated for some time. 2. In general, Republicans have fought attempts to strengthen gun control laws. Democrats favor stronger laws, especially with regard to so-called assault weapons. 3. Opponents cite the Second Amendment. 4. Answers will vary.

page 75, Fact and Opinion: 1. F, 2. O, 3. O, 4. F, 5. O, 6. O, 7. O, 8. O, 9. F, 10. O; Second Amendment: Answers will vary.

page 76, Read and Comment on a National News Article: Answers will vary.

page 77, Name Those Synonyms from the National Scene: Answers will vary.

Chapter 6, "World News"

page 81, Commonly Used Terms from the International News: Answers will vary

page 82, Use New Words in Sentences: Answers will vary.

page 83, Write Meanings for New Words: Definitions will vary but may be similar to the following: 1. supreme power, 2. the position of not taking sides, 3. military order to stop fighting, 4. one who moves to a new country to live, 5. To remove weapons or make them harmless, 6. the practice of conducting negotiations between countries, 7. spying, 8. a distribution of power among nations that prevents

a nation from gaining power over another,
9. Organization of Petroleum Exporting Countries, consisting of 11 nations

page 84, Read an Article about a World Event: Answers will vary.

page 85, Write a Letter to the Editor: Answers will vary.

page 86, Around the World News: Answers will vary.

Chapter 7, "Advertising"

page 91, Common Classified Ad Abbreviations: Answers will vary.

page 92, Examining a Display Ad: Answers will vary.

page 94, Deciphering Classified Ads: Answers should resemble the following:
1. 3 bedrooms, 2 bathrooms, house downtown, with wall-to-wall carpeting, central heat and air conditioning, a fireplace, and a large dining room, $1000 month
2. Like new furnished apartment, one block from the beach, 2 bedrooms, 1 bathroom, security deposit required
3. Experienced electrician wanted, either full-time or part-time, must be licensed, Equal Opportunity Employer
4. Large mobile home with 2 bedrooms and 1 bathroom, utilities included, along with a washer, dryer, and dishwasher, $800 a month
5. Renovated efficiency apartment near downtown, has new appliances, security deposit and references required.
6. Part-time desk clerk, flexible hours, experience required. $10 hour.

page 95, Write Three Classified Ads: Answers will vary.

page 96, Fill in a Venn Diagram: Answers will vary. Some possible responses include:
Classified Ads: are also called want ads; appear in a certain section of the newspaper; use many abbreviations; are short; deal with such things as jobs, real estate, garage sales, etc; are often placed by individuals.

Both: trying to sell something

Display ads: often take up an entire page; are sometimes individual inserts; usually contain illustrations; use various techniques to influence consumers.

page 97, Compare an Antique and a Modern Ad:
Answers will vary.

page 98, Write a Letter of Interest for a Job Ad:
Answers will vary.

Chapter 8, "The Sports Page"

pages 101–102, Make Sense Out of Sports' Jargon

Football Terms: 1. receiver who takes a position at the far end of the line of scrimmage, 2. end who lines up next to a tackle, 3. end lined up away from a tackle, 4. short pass thrown over rushing defensive players to a back who has lots of blocking in front, 5. play in which the quarterback rolls down the line of scrimmage with the option to run, pass, or lateral the ball to a trailing back, 6. play in which the quarterback drops back as if to pass but then hands the ball off to a back, 7. long pass thrown in the direction of the end zone, 8. play in which the bulk of the defense rushes the quarterback, 9. the playing field, 10. type of offense characterized by frequent and quick passes

Baseball Terms: 11. ball hit sharply, usually low and in a nearly straight line, 12. a fly ball hit lightly that falls between the infield and outfield, 13. third base position, 14. minor league team, 15. bunting to score a runner from third base, 16. the pitcher and catcher, 17. when the batter is safe at first on a ground ball because the infielder threw to another base to force out a runner, 18. when the runner is out on a bunt or a fly ball but a runner advances or runners advance, 19. in the American League, a player whose only role in the game is to bat for the pitcher without causing the pitcher to be removed from the game, 20. a pitch thrown deliberately near the head of a batter to intimidate him

Basketball Terms: 21. when a defensive player interferes with a shot while the ball is above the rim on its downward arc, 22. a foul assessed against a coach or player for rough play or unacceptable language or behavior, 23. defensive players guarding the opposition very closely as the ball is advanced down the court, 24. a missed shot that doesn't touch the rim or the backboard, 25. a missed shot that hits the backboard but not the rim, or just a very bad shot, 26. when the offense dribbles and passes to use up as much time as possible rather than to score, 27. a defense in which players guard a certain area of the court rather than an individual player, 28. to pass or throw the ball to another player who scores, 29. situation in which a player is awarded a second free throw if he makes the first, 30. a clock indicating how many seconds the offensive team has left to take a shot,

31. when a player positions his body in front or back of an opponent to allow a teammate an uncontested shot, 32. the offensive team's defensive end of the court

page 104, Analyze the Pre-Game Story: 1. The article is about football. Clues include the high scores, quarterback, completing passes, wide receiver, touchdowns, linebacker. 2. Frostburg and Sleetville, 3. juggernaut: something that destroys everything in its path; donnybrook: a riot or brawl; 4. "Rifle" Timmons has a strong passing arm; "Blue Streak" Otis is a fast runner; "Bull" Bevins: is powerful and fearsome; "Truck" Timmons is large and powerful like a truck, 5. Answers will vary.

page 105 Answer Questions About a Sports Story: Answers will vary.

Chapter 9, "Television and Entertainment"

page 109, Comment on a Celebrity Story: Answers will vary.

page 110, Analyze a Movie Review: 1. Attack of the Alien Broccoli; 2. Freddy Flick; 3. The movie is about broccoli clusters from another planet who attack kids for saying bad things about broccoli. 4. No, the reviewer gave it one star. He said, "give me a break" and "save your money," and "avoid this no-brainer." 5. Answers will vary.

page 111, Critique a Movie Review: Answers will vary.

page 112, Pre-Review Checklist: Answers will vary.

page 114, Fill in a Venn Diagram: Answers will vary.

Chapter 10, "The Comics"

page 117, Understanding "A Brief History of the Comics": 1. February 17, 1895; 2. "Hogan's Alley", The Yellow Kid; 3. "Peanuts"; 4. "Dick Tracy"; 5. The word *comic* comes from the Greek word that means "something that produces laughter." 6. No, some are adventures, some are about daily life. 7. Answers will vary. 8. Answers will vary.

page 118, Explore a Comic Strip: Answers will vary.

page 119, Describe a Comic Strip Character: Answers will vary.

page 120, Draw a Comic Strip: Answers will vary.

page 121, Categorize Comic Strips: Answers will vary.

page 122, Identify Parts of Speech in Comics: Answers will vary.

page 123, Create a Cartoon or Comic Strip: Answers will vary.

ROOFING

Chapter 11, "Other Pages"

page 127, Skim a Gardening Article: 1. The Popular but Particular Potato; 2. Hannah Horticulturist; 3. potato; 4. in the spring when there is no danger of frost; 5. Answers will vary, but may include: not a popular crop in the home garden, certified seeds are best, garden should be weeded, and so on. 6–10. Answers will vary.

page 129, Perusing the Food Section: Answers will vary.

page 131, Commonly Used Terms from the Business News: **merger**–the combining of two or more companies or corporations; **monopoly**–control of a product or service by one company or corporation; **antitrust**–containing laws to protect against monopolies and unfair business practices; **downsizing**–reducing a business in size by eliminating jobs and/or facilities

page 132, Use New Words in Sentences: Answers will vary.

Era Works, Atlantic Docks, Brooklyn.

MANUFACTORY OF

GWYNNE'S PUMPING ENGINE,